W9-AYA-631

A CATECHISM FOR ADULTS

REV. WILLIAM J. COGAN

Also available in Spanish
"Catecismo para adultos"

CATECHETICAL TEACHING AIDS

COGAN PRODUCTIONS

FOR ADULT ENRICHMENT

555 W. Illinois Ave., Aurora, Illinois 60506

Nihil obstat
Very Rev. Noel G. Foley

Imprimatur
Most Rev. Joseph B. Brunini, D. D.
Bishop of Natchez—Jackson

June 24, 1975

Copyright 1975
by Rev. William J. Cogan
All rights reserved
12th Printing 1987

PRINTED IN THE UNITED STATES OF AMERICA

LIST OF LESSONS

INTRODUCTION

For many people God is some kind of strange Power who is somewhere in outer space. He somehow created the universe and everything in it, but He isn't interested in the people who live on this planet. This is far from the truth. In these lessons you will see how really interested God is in you and how much He loves you. The instructions you receive from the priest will help you to know and understand better God's great love for you. If you have not understood this very well before, you will come to realize how much you have missed in life and you will surely thank God for leading you to these instructions. He is doing this because He loves you.

Lesson 1: **Religion**

1. What is the purpose of these lessons?

To help supply what is missing in the lives of so many people—the knowledge and practice of true religion.

> *"The mind of the intelligent man seeks knowledge, but the mouth of fools feeds on folly"* [Proverbs 15:14].

2. Why is religion the most important study you can take up?

Because religion leads us to friendship with God now and forever, and there is nothing more valuable or more important than this.

> *"What does it profit a man if he gain the whole world, but suffer the loss of his own soul?"* [Matthew 16:26].
> *"You shall know the truth, and the truth shall make you free."* [John 8:32].

3. What is religion?

a) Acknowledging God by faith in him and believing everything He has told the human race.

b) Loving God with a wholehearted love.

c) Glorifying God by doing His will as Christ taught us by His words and example

> *"Be doers of the word, and not hearers only, deceiving yourselves"* [James 1:22].

4. Is religion really necessary?

Yes, for several reasons:

a) God, our Heavenly Father, wants every human being to follow His plan.

b) Without religion and following God's plan, life is meaningless.

> *"The supreme meaning of human life is this: to acknowledge God and to glorify Him by doing His will as Christ taught us by His words and the example of His life and thus to come to eternal life."* [General Catechetical Directory, par 41].

c) Lack of religion causes unhappiness.

"For he who despises wisdom and instruction is doomed. Vain is their hope, fruitless are their labors, and worthless are their works. Their wives are foolish and their children wicked; accursed is their brood." [Wisdom 3:11-12].

5. What will happen to those who don't practice religion?

Those who are guilty of serious neglect in this matter will go to hell.

"The Lord Jesus ... will come from heaven with the angels of His power, in flaming fire, to inflict punishment on those who do not obey the gospel of our Lord Jesus Christ." [2nd Thessalonians 1:7-8].

6. What will religion give you in this life?

God's friendship, divine adoption and a share in His life, a good conscience, and peace of mind. These are the greatest treasures anyone could have.

"Blessed are they who hear the word of God and keep it," [Luke 11:28].

"Those who love your law have great peace, and for them there is no stumbling block." [Psalm 118:165].

PRACTICAL POINTS

1. "The sad fact is that many people today pay little or no attention to God, while others are persuaded that God is distant, indifferent, and altogether absent. That is because modern life is man-centered, not God-centered." [Basic Teachings, Catholic Bishops, par. 2]

2. There have been some very good people who did not know very much about God and religion. But ignorance is not a virtue. Those good people would have loved God even more if they had known more about Him. Everything we learn about God is a further reason for loving Him. That is why the study of religion is so beautiful, so enjoyable, so interesting, so valuable.

Lesson 2: The Bible and Tradition

God, who at sundry times and in divers manners spoke in times past to the fathers by the prophets, last of all in these days has spoken to us by his Son, whom he appointed heir of all things, by whom also he made the world [Hebrews 1:1]

1. What is the Bible?

A collection of writings which were inspired by God and which contain the message of salvation.

"All Scripture is inspired by God and useful for teaching, for reproving, for correcting, for instructing in justice; that the man of God may be perfect, equipped for every good work" [2nd Timothy 3:16-17].

2. What does "inspired by God" mean?

It means that God chose some men and moved them to write down faithfully all the things, and only those things, which He wanted written down.

"For not by will of man was prophecy brought at any time; but holy men of God spoke as they were moved by the Holy Spirit" [2nd Peter 1:21].

3. Who, then, is the real author of the Bible?

God is, since He moved these men to write down the things He ordered, although He allowed them to write in their own language and style.

"For I give you to understand, brethren, that the gospel which was preached by me is not mine. For I did not receive it from man, nor was I taught it; but I received it by a revelation of Jesus Christ" [Galatians 1:11-12].

4. When were all these writings put together?

The Church put all of them in one book between the years 350 and 405.

5. How is the Bible divided?

It is divided into two main parts, the Old Testament (Hebrew) and the New Testament.

6. What is contained in the Old Testament?

The Old Testament contains the things God told the human race from the beginning of the world up to the coming of His Son, Jesus Christ.

7. What is contained in the New Testament?

The New Testament contains what God has told us through His Son and through His Apostles and others.

8. Is it possible to misunderstand the Bible?

Yes, even the Bible itself says so.

"In these epistles there are certain things difficult to understand, which the unlearned and the unstable distort, just as they do the rest of the Scriptures also, to their own destruction" [2nd Peter 3:16].

9. Do we get from the Bible alone all our knowledge and certainty about what God has told us?

No, there is also Sacred Tradition.

"Many other signs also Jesus worked in the sight of his disciples, which are not written in this book" [John 20:30].

10. What is Tradition?

The Word of God handed on to us by the Apostles in their preaching and by their successors in the Church to the present day.

"So, then, brethren, stand firm, and hold the teachings that you have learned, whether by word or by letter of ours" [2nd Thessalonians 2:15].

11. Do you have to believe in Tradition?

Yes, because Tradition hands on in its full purity God's word. Sacred Tradition together with Sacred Scripture form one sacred deposit of the word of God.

The early Christians learned everything by Tradition, since only later on were some of the teachings of Jesus written down, the last writing being done at the end of the first century.

12. Are we permitted to believe whatever we want?

No, we are obliged to accept all the truths contained in the Bible and Tradition, since this is how God speaks with us as His friends. Saying "No" here is saying "No" to God.

"The Lord Jesus ... will come from heaven with the angels of his power, in flaming fire, to inflict punishment on those who do not know God, and who do not obey the gospel of our Lord Jesus Christ" [2nd Thessalonians 1:7-8].

13. How can we come to know and understand the right meaning of God's word?

The task of officially explaining the meaning of the word of God in the Bible and Tradition has been entrusted to the living teaching Church which our Lord founded.

PRACTICAL POINTS

1. "Earthly matters and the concerns of faith derive from the same God." [Vatican Council II *The Church Today*, par. 36] There can be no contradiction between the Bible and Science since both are concerned with unchangeable Truth. The story of the creation of the world and the human race, for example, was not intended by God to be a scientific explanation, but merely a simple way of instructing uneducated people.

2. "Ignorance of the Scriptures is ignorance of Christ." [St. Jerome]

3. Many people buy a Bible, start to read it and then quit because reading the Bible without help can be pretty discouraging. HOW TO READ YOUR BIBLE can show you how to read it and make it interesting besides. Available from the Parish Book Store or Cogan Productions, 555 W. Illinois Ave., Aurora, Ill. 60506.

NOTES

_____

_____

_____

_____

Lesson 3: **God and the Holy Trinity**

Oh, the depth of the riches of the wisdom and of the knowledge of God! How incomprehensible are his judgments and how unsearchable his ways! For who has known the mind of the Lord, or who has been his counsellor? Or who has first given to him, that recompense should be made him? For from him and through him and unto him are all things. To him be the glory forever, amen [Romans 11:33-36]

1. Who is God?

God is the Creator "who made heaven and earth, the sea, and all that is in them" [Psalm 146:6].

2. What does "creator" mean?

It means that God made all things out of nothing.

> *"I beseech thee, my son, look upon heaven and earth, and all that is in them, and consider that God made them out of nothing, and mankind also" [2nd Machabees 7:28].*

3. What is a creature?

A creature is anything made by God.

4. How do you know there is a God?

If you just examine the things in this world, you have to admit that someone had to make them.

> *"But now ask the beasts to teach you, and the birds of the air to tell you; or the reptiles on earth to instruct you, and the fish of the sea to inform you. Which of all these does not know that the hand of God has done this?" [Job 12:7-9].*
>
> *"The fool says in his heart, 'There is no God' " [Psalm 13:1].*

5. Why can't you see God?

Because He has no body.

> *"God is spirit" [John 4:24].*

6. Where is God?

God is everywhere.

> *"Where can I go from your spirit? From your presence where can I flee? If I go up to the heavens, you are there; if I sink to the nether world, you are present there" [Psalm 138:7-8].*

7. Does God see and know all things?

Yes, because He is personally present everywhere. This is a very consoling fact.

"The eyes of the Lord are in every place, keeping watch on the evil and the good" [Proverbs 15:3].

8. How old is God?

We cannot measure God's age. He always is and always was and always will be, without change. This is what it means to be eternal.

"Before the mountains were begotten and the earth and the world were brought forth; from everlasting to everlasting you are God" [Psalm 89:2].

9. Can God do all things?

Yes, "with God all things are possible" [Matthew 19:26].

10. Is God Alive?

Yes, God is alive; He is the source of all life.

11. Is God dependent on anyone or anything or is He imperfect in any way?

No, He is independent and absolutely perfect in every way and without limits of any kind. We call this: infinite perfection.

"Neither is he served by human hands as though he were in need of anything, since it is he who gives to all men life and breath and all things" [Acts 17:25].

12. Is God interested in you?

Yes, and He loves you personally with an unlimited love.

"Can a woman forget her infant, so as not to have pity on the son of her womb? And if she should forget, yet will not I forget thee" [Isaias 49:15].

13. Does God's love include forgiveness of all your sins?

Yes, if you are truly sorry for them.

"For the Lord your God is merciful, and will not turn away his face from you, if you return to him" [2nd Paralipomenon 30:9].

14. What do we mean by the Holy Trinity?

This means that there are three persons in One God.

"Go, therefore, and make disciples of all nations, baptizing them in the name of the Father, and of the Son, and of the Holy Spirit" [Matthew 28:19].

15. Who are the three Persons in God?

God the Father, God the Son and God the Holy Spirit.

"For there are three that bear witness in heaven: the Father, the Word, and the Holy Spirit; and these three are one" [1st John 5:7].

16. Are the three Persons of the Holy Trinity equal?

Yes, They are equal, but each is a distinct person, and each is truly God, truly divine.

17. Can we understand this truth about the inner life of God?

This is a mystery that no human mind can completely understand.

PRACTICAL POINTS

1. There are many things in this world which the human mind cannot understand, such as growth, sight, hearing, electricity. Therefore, we should not be surprised to find that we cannot completely understand the God who made the world.

2. If God had not told us this, we would never have known that there is this community of persons within the one divine nature. God revealed to us this intimate truth about His inner life because He loves us and because He wants us through faith and Baptism to acquire a deep familiarity with the three divine Persons by being lifted up to share in their divine nature. [General Catechetical Directory, par. 47]

Lesson 4: **Prayer**

"Ask, and it shall be given you; seek and you shall find; knock, and it shall be opened to you. For everyone who asks, receives; and he who seeks, finds; and to him who knocks, it shall be opened. Or what man is there among you, who, if his son asks him for a loaf, will hand him a stone; or if he asks for a fish, will hand him a serpent? Therefore, if you, evil as you are, know how to give good gifts to your children, how much more will your Father in heaven give good things to those who ask him!" [Matthew 7:7-11]

1. What is prayer?

Prayer is the raising of the mind and heart to God to communicate with Him.

2. Why should you pray?

You should pray—

a) to adore God, to tell Him that He made you and that you depend upon Him for absolutely everything.

b) to thank God for the blessings He has given you.

"What hast thou that thou hast not received? And if thou hast received it, why dost thou boast as if thou hadst not received it?" [1st Corinthians 4:7].

c) to ask God's pardon for your sins.

"O God, be merciful to me a sinner!" [Luke 18:13].

d) to ask God's help in all things.

"Ask, and it shall be given you; seek and you shall find; knock, and it shall be opened to you" [Matthew 7:7].

3. When should you pray?

Every day—

a) in the morning—to offer the day to God and ask His help in the temptations of the day.

b) during the day, especially during temptations.

c) at night—to thank God for the blessings of the day and to ask Him to forgive you for the sins committed that day.

d) before and after meals.

The prayers to be said every day are on Pages 136 and 137.

4. To whom should you pray?

a) To God the Father, Son and Holy Spirit.

b) You may also pray to the Blessed Virgin, the angels and the Saints.

"And with the prayers of the saints there went up before God from the angel's hand the smoke of the incense" [Apocalypse (Revelation) 8:4].

5. Why may you pray to the Blessed Virgin, the angels and the Saints?

Because they are God's best friends, God will listen to them more than to us who are still sinners.

"Go to my servant Job, and offer up a holocaust for yourselves; and let my servant Job pray for you; for his prayer I will accept not to punish you severely. For you have not spoken rightly concerning me, as has my servant Job" [Job 42:8-9].

6. For whom should you pray?

a) For everyone on earth including your enemies.

"But I say to you, love your enemies, do good to those who hate you, and pray for those who persecute and calumniate you" [Matthew 5:44].

b) For the souls in Purgatory (see Lesson 12).

7. What should you pray for?

Every day pray to get into heaven; when praying for anything else, always say, "If it is your will, Lord."

"For after all these things the Gentiles seek; for your Father knows that you need all these things. But seek first the kingdom for God and his justice, and all these things shall be given you besides" [Matthew 6:32-33].

8. Does God always hear your prayers?

Yes, but He does not always give what you ask for, because you do not always know what is good for you, and sometimes ask for things that are bad for you.

9. Does God hear the prayers of sinners?

Yes, whenever they with faith sincerely ask for His help.

"But the tax collector, standing far off, would not even lift up his eyes to heaven, but beat his breast, saying, 'God be merciful to me a sinner!' I tell you this man went down to his house justified." [Luke 18:13-14].

10. How should you pray?

a) With *attention,* keeping your mind on your prayer.

b) With *humility,* realizing that you are powerless without God.

c) With *confidence* realizing that God can do all things.

d) With *perseverance,* without giving up hope.

"The confidence that we have towards him is this, that if we ask anything according to his will, he hears us" [1st John 5:14].

11. Why is public community prayer necessary?

Because as members of human society, we owe God public recognition of Him as Supreme Master of society.

12. How does public community prayer help the world?

By demonstrating the great Christian ideal of the brotherhood of man in uniting men and women of all ages, all races and all places in life in the worship of our heavenly Father.

13. Why should a family pray together?

a) To ask God to bless them as a family.

b) To imitate the Holy Family (Jesus, Mary and Joseph).

c) To give good example to the children.

d) To keep the family together.

"For where two or three are gathered together for my sake, there am I in the midst of them" [Matthew 18:20].

14. How often should a family pray together?

At least once a day, preferably after the evening meal, when all the members of the family are together.

"A family that prays together stays together" [Father Peyton].

15. Why do Catholics have statues and pictures of the Saints?

a) Because they wish to honor the Blessed Virgin and the Saints, just as we honor public heroes.

b) Because seeing holy pictures and statues of God's Saints helps us to set our minds on "things that are above" [Colossians 3:2] and thus we are helped to pray.

PRACTICAL POINTS

1. Besides formula prayers, such as the Our Father and the Hail Mary, we should pray often right from the heart in our own words. Our very best praying often is done without even putting our thoughts into words. This has been called "praying in your own words without words." Another name for this is mental prayer or meditation. Fifteen or twenty minutes of this kind of praying every day is one of the very best ways to foster friendship with Our Lord.

2. It is good to pray during the day with short prayers, such as "Jesus, I love you," "My God, I offer this hour of work for my sins," "My Jesus, mercy."

3. It is not necessary to kneel while praying, but it certainly does help to create the right attitude and spirit of prayer to kneel when praying especially, for example, during your morning and night prayers.

NOTES

_____

_____

_____

_____

_____

_____

_____

Lesson 5: **Public Worship of God**

Note: As children of God, we are called to prayer and worship not only as individuals but as members of society, members of the human family, members of His Church. The chief form of public community worship in the Catholic Church is the Holy Sacrifice of the Mass. A fuller explanation will be given in Lesson 22. A few introductory ideas are given here for those who wish to start attending Mass at this early stage in their instructions.

1. What happens at Mass?

Bread and wine are changed into the Body and Blood of Christ and offered to God as a sacrifice as Jesus offered Himself upon the cross

2. Who offered the first Mass?

Jesus Christ, at the Last Supper on the night before He died, nearly 2000 years ago.

> *"And while they were at supper, Jesus took bread, and blessed and broke, and gave it to his disciples, and said, 'Take and eat; this is my body. 'And taking a cup, he gave thanks and gave it to them, saying, 'All of you drink of this; for this is my blood' "*
> *[Matthew 26:26].*

3. How could Jesus change bread and wine into His Body and Blood?

By His divine power; He is God, as will be shown in Lesson 15.

4. Did Jesus ever give this power to anyone else?

Yes, to His twelve Apostles.

> *"Do this in remembrance of me" [Luke 22:19].*

5. Did Jesus want His Apostles to hand down this power to others?

Yes, because He wanted all men of all times to participate actively in this sacrificial offering and in the communion, the eating and drinking, of the spiritual food which is truly His Body and Blood.

"Unless you eat the flesh of the Son of Man, and drink His blood, you shall not have life in you" [John 6:54].

6. How did the Apostles hand down this power?

By making other men priests and bishops (see Lesson 27).

7. Who has this power today?

The priests and bishops of the Catholic Church.

8. At what part of the Mass does the priest change bread and wine into the Body and Blood of Jesus Christ?

At the part called the consecration, toward the middle of the Mass, when he says, "This is My Body; this is My Blood."

PRACTICAL POINTS

1. If there are a number of things which you don't understand when you attend Holy Mass at this stage of your instruction, be patient. Join in the prayers and ask God for strong faith as we go through the lessons leading to Lesson 22.
2. For now, read and reread the sixth chapter of the Holy Gospel according to St. John.

NOTES

_____

_____

_____

_____

_____

_____

_____

_____

Lesson 6: Angels and Devils

And I beheld, and I heard a voice of many angels round about the throne, and the living creatures and the elders, and the number of them was thousands of thousands, saying with a loud voice, "Worthy is the Lamb who was slain to receive power and divinity and wisdom and strength and honor and glory and blessing." [Apocalypse (Revelation) 5:11-12]

1. What is an angel?

An angel is a spirit, that is, a person who does not have a body.

2. Is an angel a real person?

Yes, because an angel has a mind as well.

3. How do you know there are angels?

The Bible mentions angels about three hundred times.

4. Why did God create the angels?

To serve Him in heaven, to act as His messengers to man and to act as guardians over human beings.

5. Do we have guardian angels?

Yes, God appoints angels to watch over every human being. It is most probable that each person has his own individual guardian angel.

> *"See that you do not despise one of these little ones; for I tell you, their angels in heaven always behold the face of my Father in heaven" [Matthew 18:10].*

6. What does your guardian angel do for you?

Your angel prays for you, protects you from evil and inspires you to do good.

> *"See, I am sending an angel before you, to guard you on the way and bring you to the place I have prepared. Be attentive to him and heed his voice" [Exodus 23:20-21].*

20

7. Did all the angels obey God?

No, some of them, led by Lucifer, or Satan, disobeyed God and were sent immediately into hell. These are the fallen angels or devils.

"And there was a battle in heaven; Michael and his angels battled with the dragon, and the dragon fought and his angels. And they did not prevail, neither was their place found any more in heaven" [Apocalypse (Revelation) 12:7-8].

8. Is there really a devil?

Yes, the Bible often speaks of the devil as a real person.

"And that great dragon was cast down, the ancient serpent, he who is called the devil and Satan, who leads astray the whole world" [Apocalypse (Revelation) 12:9].

9. How does the devil act toward human beings?

The devil tempts people to commit sin.

"Be sober, be watchful! For your adversary the devil, as a roaring lion, goes about seeking someone to devour. Resist him, steadfast in the faith, knowing that the same suffering befalls your brethren all over the world" [1st Peter 5:8-9].

10. How can you fight the devil?

The best weapons against the devil are prayer and sacrifice, such as fasting.

"Put on the armor of God, that you may be able to stand against the wiles of the devil. For our wrestling is not against flesh and blood, but against the Principalities and the Powers, against the worldrulers of this darkness, against the spiritual forces of wickedness on high" [Ephesians 6:11-12].

PRACTICAL POINTS

1. Your guardian angel is a real person, who is always with you to help and protect you. Pray to him often and thank him for his help. Your guardian angel is an indication of how much God loves and cares for you.

2. The devil has succeeded in getting a large number of people to think of him as a Halloween ghost. He is a real person and is a real danger to you personally.

3. Not all your temptations come from the devil. Others come from your own flesh and from the world about you.

Lesson 7:
Human Beings and the Purpose of Life

"Do not lay up for yourselves treasures on earth, where rust and moth consume, and where thieves break in and steal; but lay up for yourselves treasures in heaven where neither rust nor moth consumes, nor thieves break in and steal. For where thy treasure is, there also will thy heart be." [Matthew 6:19-21]

1. What is a human being?

A creature who has a body and a soul.

"You have made him little less than the angels, and crowned him with glory and honor" [Psalm 8:6].

2. What is the soul?

It is the spiritual part of man that will never die.

"God said, 'Let us make mankind in our image and likeness'" [Genesis 1:26].

3. Where in you is your soul?

In every part of you that is alive.

4. Is your soul real?

Yes, just as real as your body.

5. How do you know you have a soul?

You can do spiritual things—you can think, do things without being forced, refuse to do things, make things, enjoy a joke, a book or a movie, talk, work out mathematical problems.

An animal cannot do any of these things. That which makes you able to do them is your soul.

6. Where did your soul come from?

God created your soul and joined it to your tiny undeveloped body in your mother's womb.

7. How long will your soul and body stay together?

Until death, which is caused by the separation of body and soul.

> *"And the dust returns to the earth as it once was, and the lifebreath returns to God who gave it"* [Ecclesiastes 12:7].
>
> *"Watch therefore, for you know neither the day nor the hour"* [Matthew 25:13].

8. What will happen to your body when you die?

It will rot away to the earth from which it came.

> *"For dust you are and unto dust you shall return"* [Genesis 3:19].

9. What will happen to your soul when you die?

It will be judged by God and will go to heaven or to hell.

> *"It is appointed unto men to die once and after this comes the judgment"* [Hebrews 9:27].

10. Will your soul ever be joined to your body again?

Yes, on Judgment Day God will call your body back from the earth and join it to your soul. This is the Resurrection.

> *"Behold, I tell you a mystery: we shall all indeed rise, but we shall not all be changed—in a moment, in the twinkling of an eye, at the last trumpet. For the trumpet shall sound, and the dead shall rise incorruptible"* [1st Corinthians 15:51-52].

11. After the Resurrection, will your soul and body be always together?

Yes, both body and soul will be together forever, either in heaven or in hell.

> *"For all of us must be made manifest before the tribunal of Christ, so that each one may receive what he has won through the body, according to his works, whether good or evil"* [2nd Corinthians 5:10].

12. When will Judgment Day be?

Nobody but God knows this.

> *"But of that day and hour no one knows, not even the angels of heaven, but the Father only"* [Matthew 24:36].

13. How should you prepare for Judgment Day?

Pray constantly, strive to grow every day in your love of God and neighbor, obey all of God's commandments, do penance for your sins.

"But take heed to yourselves, lest your hearts be overburdened with self-indulgence and drunkenness and the cares of this life, and that day come upon you suddenly as a snare. For come it will upon all who dwell on the face of the earth. Watch, then, praying at all times, that you may be accounted worthy to escape all these things that are to be, and to stand before the Son of Man" [Luke 21:34-36].

14. What, then, is the true purpose of life?

To glorify God by striving always to know and love and serve Him better and by helping others to do the same.

"For what does it profit a man, if he gain the whole world, but suffer the loss of his own soul? Or what will a man give in exchange for his soul?" [Mark 8:36].

"Behold now, you who say, 'Today or tomorrow we will go into such a city, and spend a year there, and trade and make money'; you who do not know what will happen tomorrow. For what is your life? It is a mist that appears for a little while, and then vanishes. You ought rather to say, 'If the Lord will,' and, 'If we live, we will do this or that' " [James 4:13-17].

NOTES

_____

_____

_____

_____

_____

_____

_____

_____

_____

_____

Lesson 8: Grace

And Jesus addressed them, and spoke to them again in parables, saying "The Kingdom of heaven is like a king who made a marriage feast for his son ... And the marriage feast was filled with guests. Now the king went in to see the guests, and he saw there a man who had not on a wedding garment. And he said to him, 'Friend, how didst thou come in here without a wedding garment?' But he was speechless. Then the king said to the attendants, 'Bind his hands and feet and cast him forth into the darkness outside, where there will be the weeping, and the gnashing of teeth.' " [Matthew 22:1-14]

1. Why did God make you?

God made you in order to show forth His goodness, to lead you to know, love and serve Him in this world and to share with you His happiness in heaven.

2. Are mere human beings equipped to share God's happiness?

No, because God has a completely different kind of life; not just a different way of life but a different kind.

To share in the happiness of another it is necesssary to have the same kind of life. A dog, for example, cannot enjoy a book because man has a higher kind of life than a dog.

3. How is God's life a higher kind of life than that of man?

God's life is unlimited, uncreated and independent, while human life is very limited, created by God and absolutely dependent on Him.

4. What, then, is needed to share in God's happiness?

A new kind of life called grace.

5. What is grace?

A sharing in the life of God, which raises you to God's level and gives you the power to share in His happiness.

"He has granted us the very great and precious promises, so that through them you may become partakers of the divine nature" [2nd Peter 1:4].

6. Does grace make you the same as God?

No, but it makes us new creatures, like to God, His adopted children, living on a level above merely human life and equipped to live with God in heaven.

Grace does not change us into God, because it is only a created share in His life and nature.

7. Can you go to Heaven without grace?

No, it is absolutely impossible to live in heaven without grace.

The wedding garment in the parable is grace. The banquet hall is heaven, and the king is God. The attendants are the angels, and the darkness outside is hell.

8. Is there grace in your soul when you are born?

No, human beings begin their lives without the gift of grace.

"All have sinned and have need of the glory of God. They are justified freely by his grace through the redemption which is in Christ Jesus" [Romans 3:23-24].

9. How can you get the gift of grace?

Baptism puts grace in your soul for the first time.

"Unless a man be born again of water and the Spirit, he cannot enter into the kingdom of heaven" [John 3:5].

10. Can we grow in the life of grace?

Yes, chiefly by receiving Holy Communion and the other Sacraments, and by prayer and good works.

"But grow in grace and knowledge of our Lord and Saviour, Jesus Christ" [2nd Peter 3:18].

11. Can you lose grace?

Yes, by turning away from God's love through serious sin.

"When sin has matured, it begets death" [James 1:15].

12. Can you feel grace in your soul?

No, because we cannot feel or experience through our five senses something like grace which is completely spriritual.

13. Does a religious feeling indicate grace in the soul?

No, nor does the absence of such a feeling indicate the absence of grace.

Someone being baptized with faith and true sorrow for sin can be certain from the promise of Jesus that Baptism is bringing the gift of grace, even though he experiences no religious feeling during the ceremony.

PRACTICAL POINTS

1. Since original sin came into the world, only one person, by special privilege, has begun life, from the first moment of conception, already blessed with the gift of grace. This was the Blessed Virgin Mary, the mother of Jesus. This favor is called her Immaculate Conception.

2. Serious sin causes the death of the life of grace in a person. Nothing, however, can kill the natural human life of the soul, for the soul is immortal.

3. Though it is not correct to say that grace makes us the same as God, the great St. Augustine did not hesitate to say when speaking of Jesus and our gift of grace: "God became man that men might become gods."

4. It has been said that between two persons, one of whom has grace and the other has not, there is a greater difference of worth and dignity than there is between a stone and an angel. The least share of grace has greater value than all created things. O Christian, recognize your dignity!

NOTES

Lesson 9: Heaven

Behold what manner of love the Father has bestowed upon us, that we should be called children of God; and such we are. This is why the world does not know us, because it did not know him. Beloved, now we are the children of God, and it has not yet appeared what we shall be. We know that, when he appears, we shall be like to him, for we shall see him just as he is. [1st John 3:1-3]

1. What is Heaven?

The place and state of perfect happiness with God in the next life.

"Eye has not seen or ear heard, nor has it entered into the heart of man, what things God has prepared for those who love Him" [1st Corinthians 2:9].

2. Who will go to heaven?

Only those who have grace in their souls at the moment of death.

"Then the king will say to those on his right hand, 'Come, blessed of my Father, take possession of the kingdom prepared for you from the foundation of the world" [Matthew 25:34].

3. What is the happiness of heaven?

It will consist in seeing God face to face as He really is and possessing Him in love forever and ever.

"We see now through a mirror in an obscure manner, but then face to face. Now I know in part, but then I shall know even as I have been known" [1st Corinthians 13:12].

4. Why does the life of Heaven give perfect happiness?

Because God made you for Himself in such a way that you can and will find perfect joy and satisfaction in Him alone.

"Thou has made us for Thyself, O Lord, and our hearts will always be restless until they rest in Thee" [St. Augustine].

5. Will everyone have the same happiness in heaven?

No, the happiness of some will be greater than others, but everyone will be as happy as he can be.

6. Why will some have greater happiness than others?

Because some will see God more clearly.

"For the Son of Man is to come with his angels in the glory of his Father, and then he will render to everyone according to his conduct" [Matthew 16:27].

7. Why will some see God more clearly?

Because they died with greater love of God and more grace in them.

"Each will receive his own reward according to his labor" [1st Corinthians 3:8].

8. How, then, should you spend your time on earth?

By striving to grow in grace as much as possible before you die.

"Do not labor for the food that perishes, but for that which endures unto life everlasting, which the Son of Man will give you" [John 6:27].
"Night is coming, when no one can work" [John 9:4]

9. Will there be any sorrow or pain in heaven?

No, nor will there be any sickness, temptation or sin, but complete, unending joy.

"And God will wipe away every tear from their eyes. And death shall be no more; neither shall there be mourning, nor crying, nor pain any more" [Apocalypse (Revelation) 21:4].

10. Will you know your family and friends in heaven?

Yes, and also the angels and saints.

"Therefore, you are no longer strangers and foreigners, but you are citizens with the saints and members of God's household" [Ephesians 2:19].

11. What would keep you from getting into heaven?

Dying after committing serious sin for which you have not sincerely repented.

"And there shall not enter into it anything defiled, nor he who practices abomination and falsehood, but those only who are written in the book of life of the Lamb [Apocalypse (Revelation) 21:27].

12. How often should you pray to get into heaven?

Very frequently since this is your very purpose in life.

"As the hind longs for the running waters, so my soul longs for you, O God. Athirst is my soul for God, the living God. When shall I go and behold the face of God?" [Psalm 41:2-3].

PRACTICAL POINTS

1. We get tired of good things in this world because they have only a limited amount of goodness and beauty and lovableness. Since God has all these perfections in unlimited amount, He will be for us the source of never-ending perfect joy. We will never get tired or bored in Heaven. The knowledge that it will last forever and ever will itself be another reason for joy.

2. When St. Bernadette was dying, she spoke with regret of those people who do not sufficiently desire Heaven. "As for me," she said, "that will not be my case. Let us determine to go to Heaven. Let us work for it, suffer for it. Nothing else matters."

NOTES

Lesson 10: Mortal and Venial Sin

Let no man say when he is tempted, that he is tempted by God; for God is no tempter to evil, and he himself tempts no one. But everyone is tempted by being drawn away and enticed by his own passion. Then when passion has conceived, it brings forth sin; but when sin has matured, it begets death. [James 1:13-15]

1. What is sin?

Sin is any thought, word, desire, action or neglect forbidden by the law of God.

2. When are you guilty of sin?

To be guilty—

a) you must realize that you are breaking God's law, and

b) you must freely choose to do it.

3. How many kinds of sin are there?

Two kinds of personal sin—mortal and venial. See Lesson 13 about Original Sin.

4. What is mortal sin?

A big sin, a serious violation of God's law.

Examples: Adultery, stealing something expensive, complete drunkenness.

5. What does mortal sin do to you?

It kills the life of grace in you.

"What fruit had you then from those things of which you are now ashamed? For the end of these things is death" [Romans 6:21].

6. Where do you go if you die in mortal sin?

You will go to hell forever.

"Their portion shall be in the pool that burns with fire and brimstone, which is the second death" [Apocalypse (Revelation) 21:8].

7. Can all mortal sins be forgiven?

Yes, if you are truly sorry for them and do everything necessary for forgiveness.

"If we acknowledge our sins, he is faithful and just to forgive us our sins and to cleanse us from all iniquity" [1st John 1:9].

8. What is venial sin?

A less serious violation of God's law, an offense not serious enough to break off friendship with God.

Examples: Impatience, ordinary anger, stealing something cheap.

9. What does venial sin do to you?

It does not take away or lessen grace in you, but it helps to cool the fervor of your love for God and to dispose you to compromise in the struggle to avoid mortal sins.

10. Where will you go if you die in venial sin?

Before going to Heaven, you must go to Purgatory.

11. Can a number of venial sins ever add up to mortal sin?

No, never.

12. If you do something wrong, but don't know it is wrong, are you guilty of sin?

No, if your ignorance or memory lapse is not your fault.

13. Are you guilty of sin if you intend to do something wrong, even though you don't actually do it?

Yes, because the intention to offend God is in itself a sin.

Example: You intend to rob a bank but are frightened away by the guards.

14. What should you do when in doubt whether or not something is sinful or whether or not it is seriously sinful?

You must make an honest effort to solve the doubt before you act; deliberately acting in such a doubt shows a blameworthy carelessness about offending God.

15. What is temptation?

Temptation is an attraction to commit sin.

16. Can you always overcome temptation?

Yes, because temptation invites you but cannot force your free choice; besides, God is always ready to help you in the struggle.

"God is faithful and will not permit you to be tempted beyond your strength, but with the temptation will also give you a way out that you may be able to bear it" [1st Corinthians 10:13].

17. What should you do when you are tempted?

First ask God to help you, and then get busy doing something else.

"Lead us not into temptation, but deliver us from evil" [Matthew 6:13].

18. How can you avoid temptations?

Avoid persons, places or things that can easily lead you into sin and ask God for actual graces.

19. What are actual graces?

They are helps of God which enlighten the mind and strengthen the will to do good and avoid evil.

"My grace is sufficient for thee, for strength is made perfect in weakness" [2nd Corinthians 12:9].

20. Do we sometimes resist God's helpful actual graces?

Unfortunately, yes, for we are free, and God when giving His help does not force us to respond.

"We entreat you not to receive the grace of God in vain" [2nd Corinthians 6:1].

Lesson 11: Hell

"The Son of Man will send forth his angels, and they will gather out of his kingdom all scandals and those who work iniquity, and cast them into the furnace of fire, where there will be weeping and gnashing of teeth." [Matthew 13:41-42]

1. What is hell?

The place and state in the next life where the souls of the damned suffer forever with the devils.

"If anyone does not abide in me, he shall be cast outside as the branch and wither; and they shall gather them up and cast them into the fire, and they shall burn" [John 15:6].

2. How do you know that there is a hell?

The Bible and Tradition often speak of the everlasting punishments of hell.

"Then he will say to those on his left hand, 'Depart from me, accursed ones, into the everlasting fire which was prepared for the devil and his angels.' And these will go into everlasting punishment, but the just into everlasting life" [Matthew 25:41-46].

3. Who will go to hell?

Those who die in mortal sin.

"And if anyone was not found written in the book of life, he was cast into the pool of fire" [Apocalypse (Revelation) 20:15].

4. Does anyone ever get out of hell?

No, hell is eternal, and those who go there remain forever. [See Matthew 25:41, 46.]

"And the smoke of their torments goes up forever and ever; and they rest neither day nor night" [Apocalypse (Revelation) 14:11].

5. What are the pains of hell?

Loss of God, suffering by fire, regret and the companionship of the damned.

"I go whence I shall not return, to the land of darkness and of gloom, the black, disordered land where darkness is the only light" [Job 10:21-22].

6. What is the pain of separation from God?

Eternal separation from God, the source of all love and happiness; this is the greatest sorrow and hurt in hell.

"The Lord Jesus who will come from heaven with the angels of His power, in flaming fire, to inflict punishment on those who do not know God, and who do not obey the gospel of our Lord Jesus Christ. These will be punished with eternal ruin, away from the face of the Lord and the glory of His power" [2nd Thessalonians 1:7-9].

7. Is there real fire in hell?

Yes, Jesus often spoke of the "unquenchable fire" of hell and says that the damned souls will be "salted with fire" [Mark 9:43], which is "everlasting fire" [Matthew 25:41].

"If anyone does not abide in me, he shall be cast outside as the branch and wither; and they shall gather them up and cast them into the fire, and they shall burn" [John 15:6].

8. How does the fire in hell differ from the fire here on earth?

The fire in hell burns without consuming and can torture not only the body but the soul as well.

9. What is the pain of regret?

It is the eternal bitter remorse from the thought that in spite of so many chances and helps given to you by God to save your soul you lost heaven through your very own fault.

10. What is the pain of the companionship of the devils?

The misery of eternal association with the devils and the most evil persons that lived on the earth, a society of mutual hatred; hell is the place in which there is no love.

"I go whence I shall not return, to the land of darkness and of gloom, the black, disordered land where darkness is the only light" [Job 10:21-23].

11. Are the pains of hell the same for all?

All those in hell will have the same kind of just punishment, but the degree of suffering will differ according to their sins and guilt.

PRACTICAL POINTS

1. Think often of hell and the possibility of your going there. Pray every day that you will not die with mortal sin on your soul. Say the Act of Contrition every night (Page 134).

2. Presumption is a sin against Christian hope which distorts the true notion of God's mercy. The presumptuous person refuses to take God at His word concerning the punishment of sinners. He foolishly expects that God will somehow show him mercy even if it means a compromise of God's own holy justice. The sin of presumption is an insult to the good God and His divine mercy.

3. Even if you are living a good life and have a well-founded humble hope of escaping hell, it is still a good thing to meditate often on this subject. It can make you a good missionary always ready to work and pray and sacrifice to save others from going to hell.

NOTES

Lesson 12: **Purgatory**

And the day following, Judas came with his company to take away the bodies of them that were slain and to bury them with kinsmen in the sepulchres of the fathers. And they found under the coats of the slain some of the donaries of the idols of Jamnia, which the law forbiddeth to the Jews; so that all plainly saw, that for this cause they were slain. Then they all blessed the just judgment of the Lord, who had discovered the things that were hidden. And so betaking themselves to prayers they besought him that the sin which had been committed might be forgotten. But the most valiant Judas exhorted the people to keep themselves from sin, forasmuch as they saw before their eyes what had happened because of the sins of those that were slain. And making a gathering, he sent twelve thousand drachmas of silver to Jerusalem for sacrifice to be offered for the sins of the dead, thinking well and religiously concerning the resurrection (For if he had not hoped that they that were slain should rise again, it would have seemed superfluous to pray for the dead). And because he considered that they who had fallen asleep with godliness had great grace laid up for them. It is therefore a holy and wholesome thought to pray for the dead, that they may be loosed from sins. [2nd Machabees 12:39-46]

1. What is purgatory?

A place and state of temporary punishment after death.

Hell, on the other hand, is a place of eternal or everlasting punishment.

2. What does the word "purgatory" mean?

It refers to cleansing: purgatory is a place where the soul is cleansed of the effects of sin.

3. How do we know there is a purgatory?

The Bible, Tradition, the constant teaching and practice of the Catholic Church, and even common sense, prove the existence of purgatory.

4. How does common sense indicate the existence of purgatory?

Only people with mortal sin go to hell, and on the other hand, no one can enter heaven with the smallest sin. There must be a place of reparation and purification for these lesser offenses and shortcomings.

5. Who goes to purgatory?

Those who have preserved the gift of grace but:

a) who die while guilty of unrepented venial sins

b) who die without having done sufficient penance to pay the debt of the temporal punishment still due their past sins.

6. What is meant by "temporal punishment due to sin"?

Even though God forgives your sins, perfect divine justice still calls for some punishment or reparation in this life or the next.

7. Is there suffering in purgatory for those who go there?

Yes, besides being temporarily deprived of their heavenly reward of union with God, those in purgatory must suffer its cleansing pains.

St. Augustine tells us that the suffering of those who are experiencing the holy cleansing fire of purgatory is more severe than anything we experience in this life.

8. How long does purgatory last for those who go there?

That depends on the number and seriousness of the sins to be atoned for.

"Amen I say to thee, thou wilt not come out from it until thou has paid the last penny" [Matthew 5:26].

9. Where do you go when you leave purgatory?

To heaven to be with God in eternal perfect joy.

"Athirst is my soul for God, the living God. When shall I go and behold the face of God?" [Psalm 41:3].

10. Can you help the souls in purgatory?

You can shorten their stay by having Masses said for them, praying for them and doing good works for them.

"Pity me, pity me, O you my friends, for the hand of God has struck me!" [Job 19:21].

11. Does the Bible say anything about praying for the dead?

Yes, we read that Judas Machabeus "sent twelve thousand drachmas of silver to Jerusalem for sacrifice to be offered for the sins of the dead" [2nd Machabees 12:43].

12. How can you avoid purgatory?

You should try, by striving to avoid every offense to God, even the very smallest, and by doing penance for sins already forgiven.

PRACTICAL POINTS

1. All Souls' Day is the day set aside by the Church for special prayers and Masses for all the souls suffering in purgatory. It is celebrated every year on November 2nd.

2. Those in purgatory cannot help themselves. We should help them by our prayers and sacrifices. As far as we know, they, in turn, can and do pray for us.

NOTES

Lesson 13: Original Sin

Through one man sin entered into the world and through sin death, and thus death has passed unto all men because all have sinned ... For just as by the disobedience of the one man the many were constituted sinners, so also by the obedience of the one the many will be constituted just. [Romans 5:12-19]

Read the first three chapters of Genesis.

1. What is Original Sin?

The sin committed by Adam, the father of the human race.

2. Who were Adam and Eve?

The first man and woman, from whom every human being on this earth is descended.

3. How did the sin of Adam affect the human race?

Because of Adam's sin, every human being is created without grace, since he was the father of the human race.

"By the disobedience of the one man the many were constituted sinners" [Romans 5:19].

4. What else did Adam's sin do?

The gates of heaven were closed; disease, pain and death came into the world; the mind of man was darkened and his will weakened.

"The inclination of man's heart is evil" [Genesis 8:21].

5. Is heaven still closed to the human race?

No, because of Christ's death on the cross, God re-opened heaven and made grace available to man.

"For as in Adam all die, so in Christ all will be made to live" [1st Corinthians 15:22].

6. What happened to the good people who died before Christ?

They went to a place of natural happiness, sometimes called Limbo, a place of rest, where they stayed until Jesus ascended into heaven.

"The poor man died and was borne away by the angels into Abraham's bosom; but the rich man also died and was buried in hell" [Luke 16:22].

7. How do you get rid of Original Sin and get grace?

Baptism takes away Original Sin and puts grace in your soul.

"Unless a man be born again of water and the Spirit, he cannot enter into the kingdom of God" [John 3:5].

8. Was any human being preserved from Original Sin?

Yes, the Blessed Virgin Mary, whose soul was created with grace in it. This is called the Immaculate Conception.

"And when the angel had come to her, he said, 'Hail, full of grace, the Lord is with thee. Blessed art thou among women' " [Luke 1:28].

PRACTICAL POINTS

1. From the way He punished the sin of Adam, we can see what a terrible thing sin is in the eyes of God. If Adam had not committed this sin, there would have been no disease, pain or death in the world and no death of Jesus on the cross.

2. Everyone is born in sin. This means that each receives a fallen human nature, stripped of the grace that once clothed it before Adam's sin, injured in its own natural powers and subjected to the dominion of death. [See Pope Paul VI, *Credo of the People of God,* par. 16]

NOTES

_____

_____

_____

_____

Lesson 14: Jesus Christ, Our Saviour

For God so loved the world that he gave his only-begotten Son, that those who believe in him may not perish, but may have life everlasting. For God did not send his Son into the world in order to judge the world, but that the world might be saved through him. [John 3:16-17]

1. Did God abandon the human race after Adam's sin?

No, He promised to send a saviour into the world and to open again the gates of heaven.

"I will put enmity between you and the woman, between your seed and her seed; he shall crush your head, and you shall lie in wait for his heel" [Genesis 3:15].

2. Who is the saviour of all men?

Jesus Christ, who, by His death on the Cross, has saved us from our sins.

"Thou shall call his name Jesus; for he shall save his people from their sins" [Matthew 1:21].

3. Who is Jesus Christ?

The Son of God, the Second Person of the Holy Trinity, true God and true man.

"And I have seen and have borne witness that this is the Son of God" [John 1:34].

4. Who is the mother of Jesus?

Mary of Nazareth, the Blessed Virgin Mary.

"And the Angel said to her, 'Do not be afraid, Mary, for thou hast found grace with God. Behold, thou shalt conceive in thy womb and shalt bring forth a son; and thou shalt call his name Jesus' " [Luke 1:30-31].

5. Did Jesus have a human father?

No, because Mary conceived her child miraculously through God's creative power.

"Therefore the Lord himself shall give you a sign. Behold a virgin shall conceive, and bear a son, and his name shall be called Emmanuel" [Isaias 7:14].

6. Who, then, was St. Joseph?

He was the husband of the Blessed Virgin Mary and the foster-father of her son, Jesus.

"An angel of the Lord appeared to him in a dream, saying, 'Do not be afraid, Joseph, son of David, to take to thee Mary for thy wife, for that which is begotten in her is of the Holy Spirit' " [Matthew 1:20].

7. Did Mary have any other children besides Jesus?

No, she and Joseph lived as brother and sister, although they were legally married.

"The angel Gabriel was sent from God ... to a virgin betrothed to a man named Joseph ... and the virgin's name was Mary ... and the angel said to her ... 'Thou shalt conceive in thy womb and shalt bring forth a son!' ... But Mary said to the angel, 'How shall this happen, since I do not know man?' " [Luke 1:26-34].

8. When and where was Jesus born?

He was born nearly 2000 years ago on Christmas Day in Bethlehem, a small town near Jerusalem in Israel.

9. Where did Jesus live during most of his life?

In the city of Nazareth, until he was about thirty years old.

10. How did Jesus spend the last three years of his life?

He preached His Gospel, worked miracles and established His church.

"And Jesus went about all Galilee, teaching in their synagogues, and preaching the gospel of the kingdom, and healing every disease and every sickness among the people" [Matthew 4:23].

11. How was Jesus condemned to death?

One of His Apostles, Judas Iscariot, betrayed Jesus to His enemies who got the Roman governor, Pontius Pilate, to condemn Him to death, as He had foretold.

"Jesus began to show his disciples that he must go to Jerusalem and suffer many things from the elders and Scribes and chief priests, and be put to death, and on the third day rise again" [Matthew 16:21].

12. What were the chief sufferings of Jesus?

The agony in the garden, the bloody sweat, the cruel scourging, the crowning with thorns, His death on the cross, His spiritual and mental sufferings.

"He was wounded for our iniquities, he was bruised for our sins. The chastisement of our peace was upon him, and by his bruises we are healed" [Isaias 53:5].

13. How did Jesus die?

He was nailed to a cross on a hill called Calvary, just outside the city of Jerusalem, and three hours later He died.

"Who himself bore our sins in his body upon the tree that we, having died to sin, might live to justice; and by his stripes you were healed" [1st Peter 2:24].

14. On what day did Jesus die?

On Good Friday.

"This is my commandment, that you love one another as I have loved you. Greater love than this no one has, that one lay down his life for his friends" [John 15:12-13].

15. When Jesus died, where did His soul go?

He went to Limbo to tell the people there that the gates of heaven would soon be opened.

"Put to death indeed in the flesh, He was brought to life in the spirit, in which also He went and preached to those spirits that were in prison" [1st Peter 3:18-19].

16. On what day did Jesus rise from the dead?

On Easter Sunday, three days after His death, as He had foretold.

"For I delivered to you first of all, what I also received, that Christ died for our sins, according to the Scriptures, and that he was buried, and that he rose again the third day, according to the Scriptures, and that he appeared to Cephas, and after that to the Eleven. That he was seen by more than five hundred brethren at one time" [1st Corinthians 15:3-6].

17. How long did Jesus stay on earth after His Resurrection?

For forty days, to prove that He really had risen and to complete His work of instructing His Apostles and founding His Church.

"To them also he showed himself alive after his passion by many proofs, during forty days appearing to them and speaking of the kingdom of God" [Acts 1:3].

18. When did Jesus ascend into heaven?

On Ascension Thursday, forty days after His resurrection.

"So then the Lord, after he had spoken to them, was taken up into heaven, and sits at the right hand of God" [Mark 16:19].

19. Who ascended into heaven with Jesus?

The people who had been in Limbo.

"Ascending on high, he led away captives; he gave gifts to men. Now this, 'he ascended,' what does it mean but that he also first descended into the lower parts of the earth" [Ephesians 4:8-9].

20. Will Jesus come back again?

Yes, on Judgment Day, to judge the living and the dead.

"For the Son of Man is to come with his angels in the glory of his Father, and then he will render to everyone according to his conduct" [Matthew 16:27].

21. What did the Apostles do after the ascension?

They went back to Jerusalem and waited for the coming of the Holy Spirit.

"But when the Advocate has come, whom I will send you from the Father, the Spirit of truth who proceeds from the Father, he will bear witness concerning me" [John 15:26].

22. When did the Holy Spirit come down upon the Apostles?

On Pentecost Sunday, ten days after the Ascension.

> *"And when the days of Pentecost were drawing to a close, they were all together in one place. And suddenly there came a sound from heaven, as of a violent wind blowing, and it filled the whole house where they were sitting. And there appeared to them parted tongues as of fire, which settled upon each of them. And they were all filled with the Holy Spirit"* [Acts 2:1-4].

PRACTICAL POINTS

1. The life of Jesus is contained in the first four books of the New Testament, called the Gospels, written by Matthew, Mark, Luke and John. However, only the main events of Christ's life are in the Gospels.

2. The brothers and sisters of Jesus mentioned in the Bible were not children of Mary but were only cousins. The words "brother" and "sister" were used by the Jews to mean cousins, because there was no word in Hebrew for cousin. [See Lev. 10:4, 1 Par. 23:22, Gen. 12:5 and Gen. 14:14.]

3. From the sufferings of Jesus, you should learn of God's great love for man, the evil of sin and the perfect example of patience in suffering. "If, when you do right and suffer, you take it patiently, this is acceptable with God. Unto this, indeed, you have been called, because Christ also has suffered for you, leaving you an example that you may follow in his steps" [1st Peter 2:20-21]. "And he said to all, 'If anyone wishes to come after me, let him deny himself, and take up his cross daily, and follow me' " [Luke 9:23]

4. "Let it then be our chief study to meditate on the life of Jesus Christ. The teaching of Christ surpasseth all the teachings of the Saints ... But he that would fully and with relish understand the words of Christ must study to conform his whole life to Him." [Thomas A. Kempis, *The Imitation of Christ*]

Lesson 15:

Jesus Christ, True God and True Man

Again the high priest began to ask him, and said to him, "Art thou the Christ, the Son of the Blessed One?" And Jesus said to him, "I am. And you shall see the Son of Man sitting at the right hand of the Power and coming with the clouds of heaven." But the high priest tore his garments and said "What further need have we of witnesses? You have heard the blasphemy. What do you think?" And they all condemned him as liable to death. [Mark 14:61-64]

1. Who is Jesus Christ?

Jesus Christ is the Son of God, the Second Person of the Holy Trinity, true God and true Man.

"But when the fullness of time came, God sent his Son, born of a woman, born under the Law, that he might redeem those who were under the Law, that we might receive the adoption of sons" [Galatians 4:4-5].

2. Is Jesus Christ really God?

Yes, He is equal to God the Father and equal to God the Holy Spirit.

"And behold, the heavens were opened to him, and he saw the Spirit of God descending as a dove and coming upon him. And behold a voice from the heavens said, 'This is my beloved Son, in whom I am well pleased' " [Matthew 3:16-17].

"Go, therefore, and make disciples of all nations, baptizing them in the name of the Father, and of the Son, and of the Holy Spirit" [Matthew 28:19].

3. Did Jesus say that He was God?

Yes, He said this to His Apostles and the people and while under oath in the Sanhedrin court.

"I and the Father are one" [John 10:30].

"But who do you say that I am?" Simon Peter answered and said, "Thou are the Christ, the Son of the living God" [Matthew 16:15-16].

4. How did Jesus prove that He is God?

Chiefly by His miracles.

> *"If I do not perform the works of my Father, do not believe me. But if I do perform them, and if you are not willing to believe me, believe the works, that you may know and believe that the Father is in me and I in the Father" [John 10:37-38].*

5. What is a miracle?

In general, a miracle is an unusual event which is contrary to or beyond the laws of nature and which cannot be explained except through the power of God.

> *"For those who believe in God, no explanation is necessary. For those who do not believe in God, no explanation is possible" [Franz Werfel in "The Song of Bernadette"].*

6. Could science in years to come explain away miracles?

Never, because only through the power of God could blindness be cured instantly or the dead come back to life just by the sound of a voice.

> *"Not from the beginning of the world has it been heard that anyone opened the eyes of a man born blind. If this man were not from God, he could do nothing" [John 9:32-33].*

7. How do miracles prove a statement to be true?

A miracle can be performed only by the power of God, and God could not perform a miracle in favor of a lie.

> *"For the works which the Father has given me to accomplish, these very works that I do, bear witness to me, that the Father has sent me. And the Father himself, who has sent me, has borne witness to me" [John 5:36-37].*

8. What were some of the miracles of Jesus?

He cured six blind men, eleven lepers, two paralytics, a deaf mute, raised three people from the dead, cast the devil out of many, changed water into wine, calmed a storm, walked on the waters of the sea, twice fed thousands of people with a few loaves of bread and a few fish—a word, a look, a gesture, a simple touch, and all nature obeys Him as Master.

> *"Many other signs also Jesus worked in the sight of his disciples, which are not written in this book. But these are written that you may believe that Jesus is the Christ, the Son of God, and that believing you may have life in his name" [John 20:30-31].*

9. What was the greatest miracle of Jesus?

His resurrection from the dead, as He had foretold.

"To them also he showed himself alive after his passion by many proofs, during forty days appearing to them and speaking of the kingdom of God" [Acts 1:3].

10. In what other ways did Jesus prove that He was God?

By the holiness of His life, by the perfection of His teaching, by His prophecies and by fulfilling the prophecies of the Old Testament.

11. What is a prophecy?

A sure foretelling of a future event which cannot be naturally foreseen but only through the power of God.

12. Were the prophecies of the Old Testament fulfilled in Jesus?

Yes, some of them were about his origin, nationality, tribe, divinity, time and place of His birth, the virginity of His mother, His flight into Egypt, His betrayal, and practically all the details of His sufferings and death, agony, scourging, mockery, crucifixion, burial and resurrection.

13. What are some of the prophecies made by Jesus?

The following have already been fulfilled: those about His passion, death, resurrection, denial by Peter, betrayal of Judas, the coming of the Holy Spirit, the persecution of His followers, the destruction of the temple and Jerusalem and the preaching of the Gospel throughout the whole world.

14. What value do these prophecies have?

Like the miracles, they prove that Jesus was telling the truth when He said He was God.

"The works that I do in the name of my Father, these bear witness concerning me" [John 10:25].

15. Is Jesus a real man?

Yes, because He has a body and a soul.

16. Is Jesus a human person?

No, He is a divine Person, the Second Person of the Holy Trinity.

Jesus Christ has two natures, a human nature and a divine nature, and yet He is only one Person.

17. Is Jesus Christ both God and man?

Yes, He is God from all eternity but became man nearly two thousand years ago.

"For in him dwells all the fullness of the Godhead bodily" [Colossians 2:9].

18. Why did God become man?

To save man from his sins and to open again the gates of heaven.

"Jesus Christ came into the world to save sinners" [1st Timothy 1:15].

19. How did Jesus save man?

By offering His death on the cross as a sacrifice of reparation for our sins.

"You were redeemed from the vain manner of life handed down from your fathers, not with perishable things, with silver or gold, but with the precious blood of Christ" [1st Peter 1:18].

20. Are you automatically saved by the death of Jesus?

No, because His death merely makes it possible for you to be saved.

"Work out your salvation with fear and trembling" [Philippians 2:12].

21. What is necessary to be saved?

You have to be brought into spiritual contact with that saving death of Jesus by faith and Baptism and loyal membership in His Church, by love of God and neighbor proved by obedience to His commandments, by the other Sacraments especially Holy Communion, by prayer and good works and by final perseverance, that is preserving God's friendship and grace until death.

"Not everyone who says to me 'Lord, Lord,' shall enter the kingdom of heaven; but he who does the will of my Father in heaven shall enter the kingdom of heaven" [Matthew 7:21].

Lesson 16: The Church

JESUS GIVES HIS AUTHORITY TO THE APOSTLES

"Who do you say that I am?" Simon Peter answered and said, "Thou are the Christ, the Son of the living God." Then Jesus answered and said, "Blessed are thou, Simon Bar-Jona, for flesh and blood has not revealed this to thee, but my Father in heaven. And I say to thee, thou art Peter, and upon this rock I will build my Church, and the gates of hell shall not prevail against it." [Matthew 16:16-18]

And Jesus drew near and spoke to them saying, "All power in heaven and on earth has been given to me. Go, therefore, and make disciples of all nations, baptizing them in the name of the Father, and of the Son, and of the Holy Spirit, teaching them to observe all that I have commanded you; and behold, I am with you all days, even unto the consummation of the world." [Matthew 28:18-20]

1. Did God intend that the Bible alone should be the guide to salvation?

No, because certain things in the Bible can be misunderstood, and because the Bible does not have everything God taught.

"This, then, you must understand first of all, that no prophecy of Scripture is made by private interpretation" [2nd Peter 1:20].
"There are certain things difficult to understand, which the unlearned and the unstable distort, just as they do the rest of the Scriptures also" [2nd Peter 3:16].

2. What did Jesus do to make sure that His teaching would never be misunderstood?

He established a church.

"The house of God, which is the Church of the living God, the pillar and mainstay of the truth" [1st Timothy 3:14].

3. When did Jesus establish His church?

Nearly two thousand years ago.

4. How many churches did Jesus establish?

Only one.

"Upon this rock I will build my church" [Matthew 16:18].
"There shall be one fold and one shepherd" [John 10:16].

5. How long did Jesus want His church to last?

Until the end of the world.

"I am with you all days, even unto the consummation of the world" [Matthew 28:20].

6. Can you find and recognize His church in modern times?

Yes, it is the church with a direct line to the Apostles in its history and its authority; it is universal and holy and has unity; it cannot teach error and cannot be destroyed.

"Teaching them to observe all that I have commanded you" [Matthew 28:20].

7. Is there only one church that has these qualities?

Yes, only the Catholic Church.

"He who hears you, hears me; and he who rejects you, rejects me; and he who rejects me, rejects him who sent me" [Luke 10:16].

8. Why is a direct connection with His Apostles so important?

It was to the Apostles that He gave the authority to rule and teach.

"As the Father has sent me, I also send you." [John 20:21].

"All power in heaven and on earth has been given to me. Go, therefore, and make disciples of all nations ... teaching them to observe all that I have commanded you." [Matthew 28:18-20].

9. Why is the church of Jesus called "Catholic"?

Because His church is for all people of all nations and all times and teaches all the doctrines of Jesus. Catholic means universal, embracing all.

10 .When was the name "Catholic" first used of the church of Jesus?

In the year 110, by St. Ignatius of Antioch, who wrote: "Where Jesus Christ is, there is the Catholic Church" [Ad Smyr. 8:2]

"The Church is called Catholic by all her enemies, as well as by her own children. Heretics and schismatics can call the Church by no other name than Catholic, for they would not be understood, unless they used the name by which the Church is known to the whole world" [St. Augustine, 4th Century, in DeVera Religione].

11. Is the Catholic Church spread all over the world?

Yes, its 840,000,000 members are from all races and colors in all sections of the world.

The marvelous growth of the Church, in spite of great obstacles and fierce persecution, is certainly a sign that it is the Church of Jesus.

12. Why do we say that the Catholic church is holy?

a) its Founder, Jesus Christ, is holy

b) it teaches a holy doctrine

c) it gives its members what is needed to lead a holy life

d) thousands of its members from every walk of life, every race and every period of history have become saints.

13. What is meant by the unity of the Catholic Church?

Unity means that all Catholics all over the world—

a) believe the same things

b) obey the same laws

c) receive the same Sacraments

d) are all united under the authority of the Pope.

"Yet not for these only do I pray, but for those also who through their word are to believe in me, that all may be one, even as thou, Father, in me and I in thee; that they also may be one in us" [John 17:20-21].

14. Why cannot the Catholic Church ever teach error?

The Bible calls the church the Body of Christ. If the church could make a mistake in its official teaching, it could rightly be said that Jesus was teaching error. So God prevents this by His special help.

15. Can we say that when the church teaches (official doctrines of faith and morals) it is still Christ teaching in the world?

Yes, because:

a) In a true sense, the church is Christ's other self.

St. Paul calls the church "Christ". [I Corinthians 12:12].
Jesus Himself identifies with His church and refers to it as "Me." [Acts 9:4],

b) Jesus said that in listening to His church we are listening to Him.

"He who hears you, hears me; and he who rejects you rejects me" [Luke 10:16].

16. What special gift did Jesus give to His church to guarantee against error?

He sent the Holy Spirit, the Third Person of the Blessed Trinity, to dwell in the church and in its members and to guide the church to the fullness of truth.

"Do you not know that you are the temple of God and that the Spirit of God dwells in you?" [I Corinthians 3:16].

"When He, the Spirit of truth, has come, He will teach you all the truth" [John 16:13].

17. Why can't the Catholic Church ever be destroyed?

Because Jesus promised that "the gates of hell shall not prevail against it" [Matthew 16:18].

"The God of heaven will set up a kingdom that shall never be destroyed" [Daniel 2:44].

18. Is there an obligation to belong to the Catholic Church?

Yes, it is a kind of sacrament or sign of intimate union with God and the instrument established by Jesus for uniting us to Him as our personal Saviour.

"Whosoever, therefore, knowing that the Catholic Church was made necessary by God through Jesus Christ, would refuse to enter her or to remain in her could not be saved" [Vatican Council II, The Church, par. 14].

PRACTICAL POINTS

1. The Catholic church accepts members of other Christian churches with respect and affection as brothers. We believe that all who believe in Jesus Christ and have been properly baptized have been in fact already brought into a certain, though incomplete, union with the Catholic Church.

2. "Nevertheless, our separated brethren ... are not blessed with that unity which Jesus Christ wished to bestow on all those whom He has regenerated and vivified into one body and newness of life ... For it is through Christ's Catholic church alone, which is the all-embracing means of salvation, that the fullness of the means of salvation can be obtained. It was to the apostolic college alone, of which Peter is the head, that we believe our Lord entrusted all the blessings of the New Covenant in order to establish on earth the one Body of Christ into which all those should be fully incorporated who already belong in any way to God's People." [Vatican Council II, *Ecumenism,* par. 3]

54

Lesson 17: **The Key to Unity in the Church**

He said to them, "But who do you say that I am?" Simon Peter
answered and said, "Thou art the Christ, the Son of the living God."
Then Jesus answered and said, "Blessed art thou, Simon Bar-Jona, for
flesh and blood has not revealed this to thee, but my Father in heaven.
And I say to thee, thou art Peter, and upon this rock I will build my
Church, and the gates of hell shall not prevail against it. And I will
give thee the keys of the kingdom of heaven; and whatever thou shalt
bind on earth shall be bound in heaven, and whatever thou shalt loose
on earth shall be loosed in heaven." [Matthew 16:15-19]

1. **What did Jesus do to make sure His church would always be united?**

   He sent the Holy Spirit to dwell in His Body, which is the Church, uniting the members with one another and with Himself, the Head of the Body.

   "He has shared with us His Spirit who, existing as one and the same being in the head and in the members, vivifies, unifies, and moves the whole Body." [Vatican Council II, the Church, par. 7]

   "Preserve the unity of the Spirit in the bond of peace: one body and one Spirit, even as you were called in one hope of your calling; one Lord, one faith, one Baptism, one God and Father of all." [Ephesians 4:3-6].

2. **Who is the chief instrument of the Holy Spirit's teaching and unifying work in the church?**

   The Pope, who is the bishop of Rome and the Vicar of Christ on earth. He is the visible head of the whole Catholic Church.

   "And I will set up one shepherd over them, and he shall feed them"[Ezechiel 34:23].

3. **Who was the first Pope?**

   St. Peter, who was made Pope by Jesus Christ Himself.

4 .**When did Jesus make Peter the first Pope?**

   Shortly before He ascended into heaven, Jesus gave Peter full authority over His whole church. Several months previously He had promised to do this.

"Thou art Peter, and upon this rock I will build My Church ... and I will give thee the keys of the kingdom of Heaven." [Matthew 16:18-19].

"Jesus said to Simon Peter, 'Feed my lambs ... feed my lambs ... feed my sheep.' "[John 21:15-17].

5. Did Peter's authority die with him?

No, it was handed down to a man named Linus, and after he died, it was handed down to another, and so on, during the past 2000 years. (See page 144)

To find Our Lord's true church in the world, you must find Peter or his lawful successor. "Where Peter is, there is the Church." [St. Ambrose, 4th Century].

6. Does Jesus require us to follow the Pope in matters of religion?

Yes, because obedience and loyalty to the Pope are among the chief requirements of Our Lord's plan for unity in His church.

"Whatever you bind on earth shall be bound in Heaven." [Matthew 16:19].

"That all may be one, even as thou, Father, in me and I in thee; that they also may be one in us. [John 17:21].

7. Can the Pope make an error when teaching religion?

Not when he is speaking solemnly (ex cathedra) as head of the church. Then he has that special protection from error which God gives as spiritual safeguard for all the members of the church.

PRACTICAL POINTS

1. The Holy Spirit dwells in the members of the church and assists them by His grace in proportion to their various tasks and offices. This is how He guides the church and gives it life and unity. "As Christ is the Head of the church, so is the Holy Spirit her soul." [Pope Leo XIII]

2. The Pope lives in Vatican City, a small independent territory within the city of Rome, Italy. He is the Bishop of Rome. Since the time of St. Peter, it is always the Bishop of Rome who is the Pope. When the Pope dies, the Cardinals elect his successor.

THE SACRAMENTS

In our natural life, we are born, we grow, we mature, we recover from illness, we are nourished. Our life of grace, in God's plan, goes along in a very similar way. In order to help us understand and appreciate this, Jesus gave us some outward signs to help us understand the spiritual life and growth of grace in us. They are called sacramental signs or Sacraments. Jesus gave us these Sacraments not only to help us understand what we cannot see but also that we might use these signs to nourish the Christian life. The Sacraments with the ceremonies that go along with them do not merely instruct us, they really do give us grace. Besides that, when we receive them worthily with faith and reverence, we are giving worship to God.

The Sacraments are another indication of how much God loves you and wants to help you to get to heaven. In the Catholic Church, therefore, it is considered to be "of capital importance that the faithful easily understand the sacramental signs and with great eagerness have recourse to those sacraments which are instituted to nourish Christian life." [Vatican Council II, *Liturgy,* par. 59]

Lesson 18: The Seven Sacraments

GETTING INTO HEAVEN IS THE ONLY THING THAT MATTERS

"Therefore, I say to you, do not be anxious for your life, what you shall eat; nor yet for your body, what you shall put on. Is not the life a greater thing than the food, and the body than the clothing? Look at the birds of the air: they do not sow, or reap, or gather into barns; yet your heavenly Father feeds them. Are not you of much more value than they? But which of you by being anxious about it can add to his stature a single cubit? And as for clothing, why are you anxious? Consider how the lilies of the field grow; they neither toil nor spin, yet I say to you that not even Solomon in all his glory was arrayed like one of these. But if God so clothes the grass of the field, which flourishes today but tomorrow is thrown into the oven, how much more you, O you of little faith!

"Therefore do not be anxious, saying, 'What shall we eat?' or, 'What shall we drink?' or, 'What are we to put on?' (for after all these things the Gentiles seek); for your Father knows that you need all these things. But seek first the kingdom of God and his justice, and all things shall be given you besides" [Matthew 6:25-34].

1. What are the most valuable things in life?

Those things which most surely increase and nourish in us the grace of God.

> *"By His power He is present in the sacraments, so that when a man baptizes it is really Christ Himself who baptizes."* [Vatican Council II, Liturgy par. 7].

2. How is the grace of God nourished and increased in us?

By those special symbolic acts of Christ in His church which are called Sacraments.

> *"The kingdom of heaven is like a treasure hidden in a field; a man who finds it ... in his joy goes and sells all that he has and buys that field."* [Matthew 13:44].

3. What is a Sacrament?

An outward sign made by Jesus Christ to give you grace. In the case of the Sacraments, the sign is an act which the church does with some ceremony and in which Christ is present by His power really doing for us spiritually what the outward action indicates.

"I came that they may have life, and have it more abundantly" [John 10:10].

4. What do we mean here by an "outward sign"?

Something which you can see (hear, feel) which tells you about or points to something you do not or cannot see.

5. How are the Sacraments outward signs?

For example, the outward sign of the Sacrament of Baptism is the washing ceremony, and it signifies the inward cleansing from sin and spiritual rising to the new life of grace which is really happening.

6. How are the Sacraments different from other outward signs?

Besides just showing or signifying that we are receiving grace, they really do give grace to us, they are not only signs of grace but are also causes of grace.

"Along with the Church, therefore, her Divine Founder is present ... in the Sacraments, infusing into them the power which makes them ready instruments of sanctification." [Pope Pius XII, Sacred Liturgy, par. 20].

7. Describe the Seven Sacraments which Jesus gave us.

BAPTISM takes away Original Sin, gives us birth in the life of grace.

CONFIRMATION, our personal Pentecost, gives spiritual strengthening.

HOLY EUCHARIST gives us the Body and Blood of Jesus Christ as our spiritual food.

PENANCE gives forgiveness of sins committed after Baptism.

ANOINTING OF THE SICK gives healing in time of serious illness.

HOLY ORDERS makes a man a priest of Jesus Christ.

MATRIMONY gives the graces needed to live a Christian married life.

8. Do the Sacraments always give grace?
Yes, if you receive them worthily.

9. Give some examples of receiving Sacraments unworthily.
Receiving Holy Communion, Matrimony, Holy Orders while in mortal sin. Not being truly sorry for or telling all your serious sins in Confession.

10. Is it sinful to receive a Sacrament unworthily?
Yes, a mortal sin; this sin is called sacrilege, abuse of a sacred thing.

11. Why are there seven different Sacraments?
Besides the giving or the increasing of grace in us, which is the effect of all the Sacraments, each Sacrament gives its own special help called sacramental grace.

> *For example, Confirmation gives you the strength to be a loyal Catholic; Matrimony gives you the special help to live your married life according to God's laws.*

12. How many times can you receive Baptism, Confirmation and Holy Orders?
Only once because the special effect of these Sacraments is permanent, and they imprint a kind of spiritual mark or character in a person.

> *Once Original Sin is removed by Baptism, it is gone forever; once a priest is ordained, he is forever a priest. The spiritual mark is indelible; after death it remains for the glory of the saved and the shame of the condemned.*

13. How many times may you receive Holy Communion and Penance?
Every day, if you wish. There are no limits on Penance. Holy Communion by general rule is received only once a day, but there are some exceptions.

> *While respecting the rules regarding frequency of Holy Communion, it is proper to say that the general ideal is to receive Holy Communion whenever you participate in Holy Mass.*

14. How often can you receive the Sacrament of Matrimony?

Only once, unless your marriage partner dies.

15. How often can you receive Anointing of the Sick?

Whenever you begin to be in danger from sickness, accident, or old age.

The Sacrament may be repeated if, after recovery, the sick person again becomes ill, or if, in the course of the same illness, the danger becomes more acute.

16. Who is the minister of the Sacraments?

a) The priest gives you Baptism, Holy Communion, Penance, and Anointing of the sick.

Anyone can baptize a person in a danger-of-death emergency situation. Also, in certain circumstances lay persons can be authorized to give Holy Communion.

b) Bishops give Confirmation and Holy Orders.

In certain circumstances, priests are authorized to give Confirmation.

c) In Matrimony, the real ministers of the Sacrament are the bride and groom.

Though necessarily present by Church law, the priest is merely an official witness.

PRACTICAL POINTS

1. The better your dispositions in receiving the Sacraments, that is, the more faith and love and sorrow for sin you have, the richer will be the effect of the Sacraments in your life.
2. After Jesus gave His Sacraments to the Church, the Church surrounded each Sacrament with beautiful ceremonies so that we can now say that each Sacrament is a celebration. These holy celebrations form part of the Church's official worship, called Liturgy.
3. Every liturgical celebration is an action of Christ the priest and of His Body the Church, a sacred action of surpassing value. That is why the Sacraments are so powerful and so necessary for a full Christian life.

Lesson 19: The Sacrament of Baptism

"Amen, amen, I say to thee, unless a man be born again, he cannot see the kingdom of God." Nicodemus said to him, "How can a man be born when he is old? Can he enter a second time into his mother's womb and be born again?" Jesus answered, "Amen, amen, I say to thee, unless a man be born again of water and the Spirit, he cannot enter into the kingdom of God." [John 3:3-7].

1. What is Baptism?

It is the Sacrament of spiritual rebirth in which we receive a share of the divine life which makes us children of God and heirs of heaven.

2. What does Baptism do for us:

a) It cleanses us from Original Sin, from all personal sins, and from the temporal punishment due to sin.

b) It makes us holy with the gifts of the Holy Spirit, especially the gift of grace.

c) It makes us living members of His Body which is the Church.

d) It brings us into spiritual contact with the saving death and resurrection of Jesus [Colossians 2:12; Romans 6:4].

e) It gives us a right and a duty to share in the work of Christ the priest, Christ the Teacher, and Christ the King.

3. Why do you have to be baptized?

Baptism is your rebirth into the life of grace; without grace you simply do not have the power to live in heaven.

"Unless a man be born again of water and the Spirit, he cannot enter into the kingdom of God." [John 3:5].

4. What kind of sin is it to delay your Baptism?

A serious sin after you have come to understand how necessary Baptism is for salvation.

"Why dost thou delay? Get up and be baptized and wash away thy sins" [Acts 22:16].

5. What do you have to do to be baptized?

a) take a course of instructions in religion and believe the teachings of Our Lord

b) repent of your sins and resolve to do your best to avoid future sins

c) have the right intention

Right intention here means you wish to do whatever God wants you to do to be saved.

6. Who gives Baptism?

Ordinarily, the priest, but anyone can baptize in an emergency.

7. How is Baptism given?

It is given by pouring water over the forehead of the person to be baptized and saying, while pouring the water, "I baptize thee in the name of the Father and of the Son and of the Holy Spirit" [Matthew 28:19].

8. What are sponsors in Baptism?

They are official witnesses, called god-parents, who assume the duty of helping their god-child remain faithful in his Catholic life.

A sponsor must be a good Catholic. A baptized and believing Christian from a separated church may act as a god-parent along with a Catholic god-parent.

9. Why do you take the name of a Saint at Baptism?

You take a Saint's name to have that Saint watch over you and to have someone to imitate.

10. Do babies have to be baptized?

Yes, because they have Original Sin, which means they have no grace.

11. How soon should a baby be baptized?

As soon as reasonably possible, certainly within the first two or three weeks after birth.

It is a serious sin to delay the Baptism of a baby for a long time.

PRACTICAL POINTS

1. An expectant mother in a non-Catholic hospital should tell the doctors and nurses that she is a Catholic and that, if there is any danger to the life of the baby, they sould send for the parish priest right away. In case of real emergency, the doctor or nurse should baptize the baby, even in the womb if necessary.

2. If there is a miscarriage, the whole substance from the womb should be put into water right away, and the words "I baptize thee in the name of the Father and of the Son and of the Holy Spirit" should be said by the one baptizing. It should be noted that the water has to flow over the skin of the fetus or embryo. Consequently, it will be necessary to break the protective membrane which encloses the body.

3. If someone who was rightly baptized in a Protestant Church wishes to become a Catholic, such a one is admitted after sufficient instruction and a profession of Catholic faith. If there is any real doubt about the correctness (validity) of the previous Baptism, before being admitted into full union with the Catholic church, the new member will receive conditional Baptism. The words will be similar to these: "If you have not really been baptized before, I now baptize you in the name of ... ."

4. Baptism calls us to a life of Christlike holiness, a life of trying to be a saint of God. In the consecration of Baptism, Christians receive "the sign and the gift of so lofty a vocation and a grace that even despite human weakness they can and must pursue perfection according to the Lord's words: 'You therefore are to be perfect, even as your heavenly Father is perfect.' " [Vatican Council II, *Priests,* par. 12]

NOTES

_____

_____

_____

_____

_____

_____

Lesson 20: The Sacrament of Confirmation

Now when the apostles in Jerusalem heard that Samaria had received the word of God, they sent to them Peter and John. On their arrival they prayed for them, that they might receive the Holy Spirit; for as yet He had not come upon any of them, but they had only been baptized in the name of the Lord Jesus. Then they laid their hands on them and they received the Holy Spirit. [Acts 8:14-18]

1. What is Confirmation?

Confirmation is the Sacrament which gives you special helps to live a good Catholic life and to profess your Christianity by word and example before the world.

Confirmation along with Baptism and Holy Communion completes your full initiation into the Christian life and the community of the Church.

2. Why is Confirmation compared to Pentecost?

When you receive this Sacrament, you receive a special strengthening from the Holy Spirit so that you may become a witness of Christ like the Apostles.

3. What are the graces of this Sacrament?

a) an increase of that grace which is a share in God's own life;

b) the sacramental grace of God's helpful strengthening for the fight against all temptations and difficulties and for the work of witnessing and defending and extending the Catholic faith and His Church.

4. Is it a sin to neglect Confirmation?

Yes, even though Confirmation is not strictly necessary for salvation, to neglect such a wonderful gift of God would surely be morally wrong.

5. Who gives Confirmation?

Ordinarily a Bishop, especially when the Sacrament is celebrated for a large group.

When adults are baptized or when already baptized adults are received into full union with the Catholic Church, the officiating priest is permitted to give them the Sacrament of Confirmation.

6. What is necessary to receive this Sacrament properly?

You must be a baptized Catholic in the state of grace and well-instructed in the Catholic religion.

7. Do you have a sponsor for Confirmation and do you take a Saint's name as in the ceremony for Baptism?

Yes, but because of the link between Baptism and Confirmation, both the original baptismal sponsor and the Saint's name are preferred as the sponsor and name for Confirmation.

8. What is expected of a confirmed Catholic?

By his good example and word and prayer and sacrifice the confirmed Catholic should take an active part in the apostolic and missionary life of the Church.

> *"On all Christians, therefore, is laid the splendid burden of working to make the divine message of salvation known and accepted by all men throughout the world." [Vatican Council II, Laity, par. 3]*

9. How is Confirmation given?

The Bishop holds his hands over those to be confirmed and prays for them. Then, putting his hand on each person, he makes the sign of the Cross on the forehead of each with blessed oil, called Holy Chrism.

10. What words does the Bishop say while he anoints with oil?

"Receive the seal of the Holy Spirit, the Gift of the Father."

11. What is Holy Chrism?

It is a mixture of olive oil and a fragrant ointment called balsam. Holy Chrism is blessed at the Bishop's Mass each year on Holy Thursday.

> *Anointing with oil is a symbol of the inner strengthening by the Holy Spirit which you receive in Confirmation.*

PRACTICAL POINTS

1. Never forget that the main purpose of the strengthening of Confirmation, which is like your own personal Pentecost, is to make you a Christian witness. "You shall receive power when the Holy Spirit comes upon you, and you shall be witnesses for me in Jerusalem and in all Judea and Samaria and even to the very ends of the earth." [Acts 1:8]

2. This call to witness, often referred to as the call to the apostolate, is your right and duty as a baptized and confirmed Catholic. "Bound more intimately to the Church by the Sacrament of Confirmation, they are endowed by the Holy Spirit with special strength. Hence they are more strictly obliged to spread and defend the faith both by word and by deed as true witnesses of Christ." [Vatican Council II, *The Church,* par. 11]

3. The witness of good example, though very valuable, is not enough. "A true apostle looks for opportunities to announce Christ by words addressed either to non-believers with a view to leading them to the faith or to believers with a view to instructing and strengthening them and motivating them toward a more fervent life." [Vatican Council II, *Laity,* par. 6]

NOTES

_____

_____

_____

_____

_____

_____

_____

_____

_____

_____

_____

_____

_____

_____

Lesson 21: The Sacrament of the Holy Eucharist

JESUS PROMISES TO GIVE THIS SACRAMENT

"I am the bread of life. Your fathers ate manna in the desert, and have died. This is the bread that comes down from heaven, so that if anyone eat of it he shall live forever; and the bread that I will give is my flesh for the life of the world".

The Jews on that account argued with one another, saying, "How can this man give us his flesh to eat?"

Jesus therefore said to them, "Amen, amen, I say to you, unless you eat the flesh of the Son of Man, and drink his blood, you shall not have life in you. He who eats my flesh and drinks my blood has life everlasting and I will raise him up on the last day.

"For my flesh is food indeed, and my blood is drink indeed. He who eats my flesh, and drinks my blood, abides in me and I in him. As the living Father has sent me, and as I live because of the Father, so he who eats me, he also shall live because of me. This is the bread that has come down from heaven; not as your fathers ate the manna, and died. He who eats this bread shall live forever." These things he said when teaching in the synagogue at Capharnaum. [John 6:48-60]

JESUS INSTITUTES THE EUCHARIST

And while they were at supper, Jesus took bread, and blessed and broke, and gave it to his disciples, and said, "Take and eat; this is my body." And taking a cup, he gave thanks and gave it to them, saying, "All of you drink of this; for this is my blood for the new covenant, which is being shed for many unto the forgiveness of sins." [Matthew 26:26-28]

1. What is the Holy Eucharist?

The Holy Eucharist is the Sacrament in which Jesus Christ is really and physically present under the appearances of bread and wine.

> *"The cup of blessing that we bless, is it not the sharing of the blood of Christ? And the bread that we break, is it not the partaking of the body of the Lord." [1st Corinthians 10:16].*

2. Why is it also called "the Blessed Sacrament"?

Because it is the most blessed of all the Sacraments, since it is Jesus Christ Himself.

3. When did Jesus make this Sacrament?

At the Last Supper, on the night before He died.

4. How could Jesus change bread and wine into His Body and Blood?

Jesus Christ is God and, therefore, can do anything.

5. Did the bread and wine change their appearance?

No, the appearances of the bread and wine (taste, smell, color, size, shape, weight) did not change, even though the bread and wine were actually changed into the Body and Blood of Jesus.

The substance of the bread and wine are changed into the substance of the body and blood of Jesus. This change is called transubstantiation.

6. Are both the Body and Blood of Christ present under the appearances of bread alone?

Yes, it is the living Christ who is present, that is, His Body, Blood, Soul and Divinity are present both under the appearance of bread and under the appearance of wine.

7. Did Jesus give anyone the power of changing bread and wine into His Body and Blood?

Yes, to His Apostles at the Last Supper, when he told them, "Do this in remembrance of me" [Luke 22:19].

8. Did Jesus want His Apostles to hand this power down to others?

Yes, because He wanted all men to eat His Flesh and drink His Blood.

"Amen, amen, I say to you, unless you eat the flesh of the Son of Man, and drink his blood, you shall not have life in you" [John 6:54].

9. How did the Apostles hand down this power?

They handed it down by making other men priests and bishops through the Sacrament of Holy Orders (see Lesson 27, Page 87).

10. When does the priest change bread and wine into the Body and Blood of Jesus?

At Mass, when he says, "This is My Body. This is My Blood."

11. What is Holy Communion?

Receiving the Body and Blood of Christ, really present in the Blessed Sacrament, as our spiritual food.

12. What is required to receive this Sacrament worthily?

No one could ever be fully worthy, but at least this much is required: you must be a baptized Catholic free of mortal sin and you must be fasting.

If someone has committed mortal sin, a sincere reception of the Sacrament of Penance [Confession] must come before Holy Communion.

13. What kind of sin is it to receive Communion unworthily?

To do so knowingly and willingly is a mortal sin called sacrilege.

"Therefore whoever eats this bread or drinks the cup of the Lord unworthily, will be guilty of the body and blood of the Lord. But let a man prove himself, and so let him eat of that bread and drink of the cup; for he who eats and drinks unworthily, without distinguishing the body, eats and drinks judgment to himself" [1st Corinthians 11:27-29].

14. What does "fasting" mean here?

Fasting to prepare for Holy Communion means not taking any food or drink, except water, for one hour before receiving Holy Communion.

For the sick and the aged confined to a hospital, their home or a home for the aged, the time of Communion fasting is reduced to approximately one quarter of an hour; and there is no time restriction at all for non-alcoholic drinks or any kind of medicine, liquid or solid.

15. How often are Catholics obliged to receive Holy Communion?

At least once a year during the Easter Season, that is, any time from the First Sunday of Lent to the Sunday after Pentecost inclusive.

16. Is this a serious obligation?

It would be a mortal sin deliberately to ignore it. This is called the Easter Duty.

17. How often do good Catholics receive Holy Communion?

Every Sunday, and many receive every day. The ideal is to receive Holy Communion every time you participate in Holy Mass, respecting, of course, the general rule allowing Holy Communion just once a day.

18. What does Holy Communion do for us?

It nourishes our Christian life, strengthens, repairs, revives, makes for growth, in general, all the things that natural food does for our body; besides, it unites us ever more closely with God and with one another.

19. Is the Blessed Sacrament in church only during Mass?

No, some of the consecrated Hosts are kept in a safe (called a tabernacle) in a prominent place in the church.

The tabernacle, therefore, is "the living heart of each of our churches". [Pope Paul VI].

20. Is the Sacrament of the Holy Eucharist important for our salvation?

Jesus said, "Unless you eat the flesh of the Son of Man and drink His blood, you shall not have life in you. He who eats my flesh and drinks my blood has life everlasting and I will raise him up on the last day." [John 6:54-55]

PRACTICAL POINTS

1. Ordinarily, we receive Holy Communion during Mass. By reasonable exception, however, we may receive in church outside of Mass or, in times of illness, at home or in the hospital.

2. Holy Communion is called Viaticum when received by someone in danger of death. This name, derived from a combination of Latin words, means that for your journey to Heaven Jesus will be "with you on the way".

3. After receiving Holy Communion, always spend some time praying to our Lord, adoring, thanking, and loving Him and asking for His help.

4. If after your last Holy Communion, you have committed some venial sins, you may nevertheless receive Holy Communion again with no obligation to confess your venial sins in the Sacrament of Penance. In your preparation for Holy Communion, you should make an Act of Contrition for these sins.

5. When you receive Holy Communion under the appearance of bread only, you do receive the living Jesus, Body and Blood. On many occasions, however, Catholics do receive Holy Communion in both forms, i.e., under the appearance of both bread and wine.

6. Some devotions in honor of Jesus in the Blessed Sacrament: Benediction of the Blessed Sacrament, Forty Hours Devotion, prayer visits to our Lord in the Church.

7. Holy Communion may be received either in the hand or on the tongue.

NOTES

_____

_____

_____

_____

_____

_____

_____

Lesson 22: The Sacrifice of the Mass

FORETOLD BY MALACHIAS THE PROPHET

From the rising of the sun even to the going down, my name is great among the Gentiles, and in every place there is sacrifice, and there is offered to my name a clean oblation, for my name is great among the Gentiles. [Malachias 1:11]

THE SACRIFICE OF THE MASS

For I myself have received from the Lord [what I also delivered to you], that the Lord Jesus, on the night in which he was betrayed, took bread, and giving thanks, broke, and said, "This is my body which shall be given up for you; do this in remembrance of me." In like manner also the cup, after he had supped, saying, "This cup is the new covenant in my blood; do this as often as you drink it, in remembrance of me. For as often as you shall eat this bread and drink the cup, you proclaim the death of the Lord, until he comes." [I Corinthians 11:23-26]

1. What is the Mass?

The sacrifice of the Cross, the sacrifice of the Body and Blood of Jesus Christ, offered in an unbloody manner under the appearances of bread and wine.

2. What is a sacrifice?

It is the offering of a gift to God by a priest and the destruction of the gift to symbolize the absolutely complete giving of ourselves to Him as our supreme Creator and Lord.

3. Were there sacrifices before the coming of Jesus?

Yes, God made Aaron and his sons priests and commanded them to offer sacrifices to Him.

"But only you and your sons are to have charge of performing the priestly functions in whatever concerns the altar and the room within the veil" [Numbers 18:7].

4. How were the sacrifices of the Old Testament offered?

Usually the priest would take an animal, offer it to God, kill it and then burn it on an altar.

5. Why were the sacrifices of the Old Testament imperfect?

They were imperfect because "it is impossible that sins should be taken away with blood of bulls and of goats." [Hebrews 10:4].

6. What was the perfect sacrifice?

Jesus offered the perfect sacrifice when He died on the cross.

"Jesus, having offered one sacrifice for sins, has taken his seat forever at the right hand of God" [Hebrews 10:12].

7. How was the death of Jesus the perfect sacrifice?

It was perfect because both the priest and victim were not only man but also God.

"But as it is, once for all at the end of the ages, he has appeared for the destruction of sin by the sacrifice of himself" [Hebrews 9:26].

8. Did Jesus want His sacrifice to be continued?

Yes, because He instituted the Mass, which is the re-presentation of His sacrifice on the Cross.

9. Who offered the first Mass?

Jesus offered the first Mass at the Last Supper when He changed bread and wine into His Body and Blood.

10. Is the Mass a true sacrifice?

Yes, it contains all the elements of a true sacrifice, priest and victim-gift and offering. By the separate consecration of the bread and wine which symbolizes His death, Jesus, the Victim of the Calvary Sacrifice, becomes truly present on the altar.

11. Is the Sacrifice of the Mass the same as the sacrifice of the cross?

Yes, they are the same in that the victim and the priest are the same, Jesus Christ.

"For as often as you shall eat this bread and drink the cup, you proclaim the death of the Lord, until he comes" [1st Corinthians 11:26].

12. What is the difference between the two sacrifices?

The difference is that the Sacrifice of the Cross was a bloody sacrifice, while the Sacrifice of the Mass is an unbloody one.

13. Did Jesus give anyone the power to offer Mass?

Yes, He gave it to His Apostles, when He said, "Do this in remembrance of me" [Luke 22:19].

"And they continued steadfastly in the teaching of the apostles and in the communion of the breaking of the bread and in the prayers." [Acts 2:42].

14. Are there men today who can offer the Sacrifice of the Mass?

Yes, the power of offering Mass has been handed down during the past two thousand years through the Bishops of the Catholic Church, in the Sacrament of Holy Orders.

15. Who is the principal priest offering the Mass?

Jesus is because He is present in the person of His minister priest at the altar, "the same one now offering, through the ministry of priests, who formerly offered Himself on the cross." [Vatican Council II, *Liturgy*, par. 7]

16. At what part of the Mass does the sacrifice itself take place?

At the *Consecration,* when the priest says, "This is My Body; this is My Blood."

17. How can you offer God the perfect sacrifice?

By taking part knowingly, devoutly and actively in the Mass, praying and singing with the others present and offering yourself to the Heavenly Father in union with Jesus the Priest and the Victim of the Sacrifice.

PRACTICAL POINTS

1. Catholics are morally obliged to attend Holy Mass every Sunday and on the six Holy Days of Obligation. Deliberately to disobey this holy commandment of the Church is a serious sin.

2. The Catholic ideal is to attend and participate in Holy Mass every day. This is especially desirable during Lent and Advent.

3. The priest may offer Mass for the souls in Purgatory. It is a custom among Catholics to have Masses said for their dead relatives and friends, instead of buying flowers. A spiritual bouquet of Masses not only helps the dead person but gives greater consolation to that person's relatives than flowers.

4. The priest may also say Mass for the intentions of the living, for example, to celebrate a wedding anniversary, a birthday, to pray for the sick, to ask for other favors, to thank God for favors received.

5. It has been the custom for centuries in the Church, when asking a priest to offer a Mass for a certain intention, to accompany the request with a gift called a Mass stipend. This is by no means a payment for the Mass but is an offering for the support of the priest.

> *"Do you not know that they who minister in the temple eat what comes from the temple, and that they who serve the altar, have their share with the altar? So also the Lord directed that those who preach the gospel should have their living from the gospel"* [1st Corinthians 9:13-14].

NOTES

_____

_____

_____

_____

_____

_____

_____

_____

_____

_____

_____

_____

Lesson 23: **The Sacrament of Penance**

When it was late that same day, the first of the week, though the doors where the disciples gathered had been closed for fear of the Jews, Jesus came and stood in the midst and said to them, "Peace be to you!" And when he had said this, he showed them his hands and his side. The disciples therefore rejoiced at the sight of the Lord. He therefore said to them again, "Peace be to you! As the Father has sent me, I also send you." When he had said this, he breathed upon them, and said to them, "Receive the Holy Spirit; whose sins you shall forgive, they are forgiven them; and whose sins you shall retain, they are retained." [John 20:19-23]

1. Why did God the Father send His Son into the world?

To save man from his sins.

> *"Thou shalt call his name Jesus; for he shall save his people from their sins" [Matthew 1:21].*

2. Does Jesus have the power to forgive sins?

Yes, Jesus has the power to forgive sin because He is God.

3. Did Jesus forgive sins while on earth?

Yes, He forgave the sins of the paralyzed man [Luke 5:18-26], the woman taken in adultery [John 8:1-11], the sinful woman [Luke 7:39-50] and the good thief [Luke 23:39-43].

4. Did Jesus give the power to forgive sin to anyone?

Yes, to His Apostles on Easter Sunday night.

> *"Whose sins you shall forgive, they are forgiven them; whose sins you shall retain, they are retained" [John 20:23].*

5. Did Jesus want His Apostles to hand down this power to others?

Yes, because He died to save *all* men from their sins.

> *"This is good and agreeable in the sight of God our Savior, who wishes all men to be saved" [1st Timothy 2:3-4].*

6. How did the Apostles hand down this power to others?

By making other men bishops and priests.

See the lesson on Holy Orders Page 87. After the apostles died, the bishops continued to hand down the power of forgiving sin, during the past two thousand years, through the Sacrament of Holy Orders.

7. Who has the power to forgive sin today?

All bishops and priests of the Catholic Church can forgive sin.

8. What is the Sacrament of Penance?

Penance is the Sacrament by which the sins committed after Baptism are forgiven and sinners are renewed in grace and reconciled with God and the Church.

9. What do you have to do to have your sins forgiven?

You have to be truly sorry for them and confess them to a Catholic priest.

"He who conceals his sins prospers not, but he who confesses and forsakes them obtains mercy" [Proverbs 28:13].

10. Why do you have to confess your sins to a priest?

This is the way Jesus Christ wants sin to be forgiven.

Otherwise, Christ would not have given men the power to forgive sin.

11. Why does the priest have to know what sins you have committed?

He has to know whether he is to forgive your sins or "retain" them. If you are truly sorry, he will forgive you; if not, he must retain them.

12. Does the priest merely pray that your sins will be forgiven?

No, acting as God's instrument and ordained minister, he truly forgives the sins. Jesus left His power of forgiveness in the Church when He said, "Whose sins YOU shall forgive, they are forgiven."

"For what I have pardoned . . . I have done it in the person of Christ" [2nd Corinthians 2:10].

13. Can you be sure that your sins are forgiven in Confession?

Yes, if you have properly confessed them and are sorry for them.

14. What does the Sacrament of Penance do for you?

Besides remitting your sins, the Sacrament—

a) restores you to the life of grace and reconciles you with God and the Church;

b) increases grace in you, if you had only venial sins;

c) gives you the strength to avoid sin in the future.

15. Can all sins be forgiven in Confession?

Yes, if you are truly sorry for them.

16. What is meant by "being sorry for your sins"?

It means that—

a) you sincerely regret having committed the sins and you detest those sins;

b) you sincerely intend not to commit those sins or any other sins in the future;

c) you sincerely resolve to stay away from any person, place or thing that can easily lead you into sin.

17. What kind of sorrow do you have to have to be forgiven?

Religious sorrow. This may be:

a) either the sincere but less perfect kind, when you are sorry for having offended God mainly because you fear the loss of heaven and the pains of hell,

b) or the perfect kind, when you are sorry for having offended God mainly because you love Him and realize that He is all good and worthy of all your love.

18. May a priest ever tell what he has heard in Confession?

No, the priest is never allowed to tell what he has heard in Confession. He must be willing to suffer death rather than break that secret. This is called the "Seal of Confession."

19. Are you obliged to confess all your sins in the Sacrament of Penance?

You do not have to confess venial sins, but you must confess all mortal sins.

20. What kind of sin is it deliberately to omit telling a mortal sin?

A mortal sin of sacrilege. After such an unworthy Confession, a person may not receive Holy Communion before returning to Confession to set the whole matter straight.

21. What should you do if you forget to confess a mortal sin?

You must tell it in your next Confession and tell the priest that you forgot it.

You may receive Communion in the meantime.

22. What do you do if you have no mortal sins to confess?

Tell your venial sins and mention some sin already told in a previous Confession.

23. How often are you obliged to receive the Sacrament of Penance?

At least once a year, if you sinned seriously.

If you ever are so unfortunate as to commit a mortal sin, say the Act of Contrition right away, and go to receive the Sacrament of Penance as soon as possible. In the meantime, you may not receive Holy Communion.

24. How often should a good Catholic receive the Sacrament of Penance?

Once a month or oftener.

NOTE

"To obtain the saving remedy of the Sacrament of Penance, according to the plan of our merciful God, the faithful must confess to a priest each and every grave sin which they remember upon examination of their conscience. Moreover, frequent and careful celebration of this sacrament is also very useful as a remedy for venial sins. This is not a mere ritual repetition or psychological exercise, but a serious striving to perfect the grace of Baptism so that, as we bear in our body the death of Jesus Christ, His life may be seen in us ever more clearly." [Rite of Penance, The Roman Ritual, 1973]

Lesson 24: Indulgences

1. What is an indulgence?

An indulgence is the taking away of all or part of the temporal punishment still due to sin.

2. What is temporal punishment due to sin?

Even though forgiveness of sins frees us from the penalty of eternal punishment in hell, divine justice requires some temporal punishment in reparation for our forgiven mortal sins and for our venial sins.

We are subject to this purifying temporal punishment either in this life or in Purgatory. An indulgence is a remission of all or some of that debt of temporal punishment. It is given as a spiritual reward for some prayer or good work.

3. What do you have to do to gain an indulgence?

You have to—

a) have no mortal sin;

b) say the prayer or do the work to which the indulgence is attached;

c) have the intention of gaining the indulgence, and

d) fulfill all the conditions laid down by the Church for each indulgence.

4. What is a plenary indulgence?

One that remits all temporal punishment.

5. What is a partial indulgence?

One that remits some of the temporal punishment.

6. What are some of the prayers and good works for which the Church grants an indulgence?

Making the sign of the cross, praying the Rosary, using holy water, making the Way of the Cross.

Lesson 25: **How to Go to Confession**

1. Examination of conscience

Kneel in church and ask God to help you know your sins. Try to remember, as well as you can, what sins you have committed since your last confession and how often you committed each one. Tell God that you are sorry for your sins. Then go to the place designated for Confession. This may be a confessional booth or a reconciliation room. You may choose to confess your sins in a face-to-face conversation with the priest or you may prefer to kneel before the confessional screen so as not to reveal your identity. A chair and a kneeling bench will ordinarily be conveniently arranged so that you can make this choice.

2. In the Confessional or Reconciliation Room

After a word of welcome from the priest, you make the Sign of the Cross. The priest will say a very short prayer encouraging you to have trust in God, and you answer: "Amen."

Then the priest may quote a few lines from Scripture (optional) which proclaims God's mercy and calls man to conversion. After this, you say:

"Forgive me, Father, for I have sinned; it is one week (or one month or whatever length of time it is) since my last Confession. I accuse myself of the following sins."

Name the sins and tell how many times you committed each one. Then say:

"I am sorry for these sins and all the sins of my whole life, especially (here name some past sin already confessed)."

The priest will then give you some prayers as penance and perhaps advise you. After this, he will ask you to express your sorrow by an act of contrition. You may use a formula prayer of contrition (see p. 137) or you may just use your own words in a brief prayer from the heart.

Then the priest will say the words of absolution and you respond: "Amen."

He will say after the absolution: "Give thanks to God, for He is good." You say in turn: "His mercy endures forever."

The priest will conclude with some expression like "Go in peace" or "God bless you." You say, "Thank you, Father," and return to your place in church.

3. After your Confession

Kneel down, say your penance and thank God for the Sacrament of Penance.

PRACTICAL POINTS

1. Remember that you have perfect freedom in the choice of a confessor. You may go to a priest who is a complete stranger to you, and there is, of course, no need to identify yourself. It makes much better sense to go to a priest who does know you and can therefore give you advice and suggestions based on this knowledge.

2. Details of our sinful acts are never mentioned in Confession except only those details that would change the nature of the sin. For example, it makes a difference whether the sin was one of thought or word or action. In a sin of impurity, it makes a difference if the persons involved are married or not. In sins of theft, the value of the object stolen makes a difference. Just telling a lie is different from telling a lie under oath.

3. Receive the Sacrament of Penance often and regularly. Some people make a very great mistake in thinking that there is no point in receiving this Sacrament unless one has committed a mortal sin. You shouldn't think of this holy sacrament as merely a way of getting rid of sins but rather as one of the very best helps given to us by Jesus to grow in deeper humble love of Him. This Sacrament brings us into personal union with the forgiving and merciful Christ, makes us grow in grace, helps us to overcome future temptations. It is difficult to lead a saintly life without receiving this Sacrament often. Receive it at least once a month. Once a week is by no means too often.

Lesson 26: **Anointing of the Sick**

Is any one among you sick? Let him bring in the presbyters [priests] of the Church, and let them pray over him, anointing him with oil in the name of the Lord. And the prayer of faith will save the sick man, and the Lord will raise him up, and if he be in sins, they shall be forgiven him. [James 5:13-15]

1. What is the Sacrament of the Anointing of the Sick?

It is the Sacrament which gives spiritual health and strength and sometimes also bodily healing to persons who are in danger of death from illness, accident or the weakness of old age.

2. How is Anointing of the Sick given?

After preparatory prayers and after laying his hands on the head of the sick person in silence, the priest anoints with blessed oil the person's forehead and hands.

3. What prayer does the priest say while anointing the sick person?

He says: "Through this holy anointing may the Lord in His love and mercy help you with the grace of the Holy Spirit. May the Lord who frees you from sin save you and raise you up."

4. What does Anointing of the Sick do for you?

The Sacrament of the Anointing of the Sick—

a) gives an increase of that grace which is a share in God's own life;

b) helps you to bear your sufferings with courage and trust in God;

c) helps you resist the temptations of the devil and anxiety about death;

d) sometimes brings about a return to physical health if it will be beneficial to the sick person's salvation;

e) completes the work of Christian penance so that if you are rightly disposed you will be ready for immediate entrance into Heaven.

5. Does Anointing of the Sick take away sin?

Anointing of the Sick takes away—

a) all your venial sins, and

b) even your mortal sins if you are unable to confess them but are truly sorry for them.

6. Who gives Anointing of the Sick?

The priest is the only proper minister of this sacrament.

7. Who may receive Anointing of the Sick?

Any Catholic in danger of death from illness, accident or the weakness of old age.

A prudent or probable judgment about the seriousness of the sickness is sufficient. A sick person should be anointed before surgery whenever a dangerous illness is the reason for the surgery. Old people may be anointed if they are in a weak condition although no dangerous illness is present. Sick children may be anointed if they are old enough to be comforted by this sacrament.

8. When should you receive Anointing of the Sick?

At the beginning of the danger, that is, as soon as the dangerous illness is recognized as such.

We should not wait until the patient is at the point of death when he may be unconscious or otherwise too weak to receive the sacrament with full attention, faith and devotion. A person with serious cancer or heart trouble, for example, should receive this sacrament even though the doctor does not anticipate death for many months or even several years.

9. How often may you receive this sacrament?

The sacrament may be repeated if you recover after anointing or if, during the same illness, the danger becomes more serious.

10. What should be done if someone dies before receiving this sacrament?

Send for the priest right away. Sometimes after apparent death, the priest may administer the sacrament conditionally.

11. What kind of sin is it to deprive a sick person of Anointing of the Sick?

A very serious sin.

It often happens that a convert is the only Catholic in the family. So, tell your relatives to send for the priest if you are ever in danger of death.

12. What should be done before the priest comes to anoint the sick person?

Spread a white cloth on a table beside the bed. Then put a crucifix, two blessed candles, a bottle of holy water, a glass of drinking water, a spoon and some cotton on the table.

A member of the family, carrying a lighted candle, should meet the priest at the door and lead him to the sick room. No one should talk to the priest, for he probably has Holy Communion with him. Everyone should kneel down when he enters.

13. What does the priest do when he enters the sick room?

After some preparatory prayers and after sprinkling the sick person with holy water, the priest administers the Sacraments of Penance, Anointing of the Sick and Holy Eucharist.

When these sacraments are given together this way to a person close to death, they are called the Last Sacraments or Last Rites of the Church. If the person has never received the Sacrament of Confirmation, the priest may give this sacrament also just before Anointing of the Sick.

PRACTICAL POINTS

1. When they are ill, even more when they are seriously ill, Catholics are happy and reassured at the arrival of the priest enabling them to receive the comforts that only the sacraments can bring.

2. If you are going to be a patient in a non-Catholic hospital, tell your parish priest which hospital and the length and time of your stay. Tell the doctors and nurses that they should send for a priest if they detect any sign of near danger of death.

3. Catholics should be buried in Catholic cemeteries. Tell your relatives to see your parish priest about your funeral.

4. The Catholic Church does not forbid cremation, although the practice of cremation is quite extraordinary and rare among Catholics.

Lesson 27: The Sacrament of Holy Orders

JESUS CHRIST THE PRIEST

Having therefore a great high priest who has passed into the heavens, Jesus, the Son of God, let us hold fast our confession. For we have not a high priest who cannot have compassion on our infirmities, but one tried as we are in all things except sin. Let us therefore draw near with confidence to the throne of grace, that we may obtain mercy and find grace to help in time of need. For every high priest taken from among men is appointed for men in the things pertaining to God, that he may offer gifts and sacrifices for sins. He is able to have compassion on the ignorant and erring, because he himself also is beset with weakness, and by reason thereof is obliged to offer for sins, as on behalf of the people, so also for himself. And no man takes the honor to himself; he takes it who is called by God, as Aaron was. [Hebrews 4:14—5:1-4]

JESUS COMMISSIONS HIS FIRST PRIESTS

And Jesus drew near and spoke to them saying, "All power in heaven and on earth has been given to me. Go, therefore, and make disciples of all nations, baptizing them in the name of the Father, and of the Son, and of the Holy Spirit, teaching them to observe all that I have commanded you; and behold, I am with you all days, even unto the consummation of the world." [Matthew 28:18-20]

1. What did Jesus do to continue His sanctifying work on earth?

To make sure that His work would be continued, Jesus established the Priesthood, through the Sacrament of Holy Orders.

"On behalf of Christ, therefore, we are acting as ambassadors, God, as it were, appealing through us" [2nd Corinthians 5:20]

2. What is the Scarament of Holy Orders?

Holy Orders is the Sacrament which gives a man the powers of the Priesthood.

3. What is a priest?

A person who offers sacrifice to God for the sins of the people.

"Every high priest taken from among men is appointed for men in the things pertaining to God, that he may offer gifts and sacrifices for sins" [Hebrews 5:1].

4. Was Jesus a priest?

Yes, Jesus was a priest.

"Wherefore it was right that he should in all things be made like unto his brethren, that he might become a merciful and faithful high priest before God to expiate the sins of the people" *[Hebrews 2:17].*

5. Who were the first Christian priests?

The Apostles, who were ordained to the priesthood by Jesus Christ Himself.

6. When did Jesus make the Apostles priests?

At the Last Supper, on the night before He died, when He gave them the power to change bread and wine into His Body and Blood.

"Do this in remembrance of me" *[Luke 22:19].*

7. Did the Apostles make other men priests?

Yes, for example, Paul, Barnabas, Timothy, Titus and Matthias.
[See Acts 13:3, 14:22, 1:24-26 and Titus 1:5.]

8. How did the Apostles ordain other men priests?

By praying for them and imposing hands on them.

"Then, having fasted and prayed and laid hands on them, they let them go" *[Acts 13:3].*

9. After the Apostles died, how were the powers of the priesthood handed down?

Before they died, the Apostles made other men bishops, who, in turn, made other men bishops, and in this way the powers of the priesthood have been handed down during the past 2000 years.

10. How are the powers of the priesthood handed down today?

Today the bishops hand down the powers of the priesthood just as the Apostles did—by praying and imposing hands.

11. What are the chief powers of the priesthood?

They are:

a) to change bread and wine into the Body and Blood of Jesus, and

b) to forgive sins.

Other powers of the priesthood are to preach with authority, administer other Sacraments and to bless people and objects.

12. Where does the authority of the priesthood come from?

From Jesus Christ, the Second Person of the Holy Trinity.

"He who hears you, hears me; and he who rejects you, rejects me; and he who rejects me, rejects Him who sent me." [Luke 10:16].

13. Who can give the Sacrament of Holy Orders?

Only a bishop.

"For this reason I left thee in Crete, that thou shouldst set aright anything that is defective and shouldst appoint presbyters in every city, as I myself directed thee to do" [Titus 1:5].

14. What is necessary to become a priest?

After graduation from college, a man has to study for about four years in a special school called a seminary, and be approved by his bishop as regards his learning, health, morals and character.

"Do not lay hands hastily upon anyone" [1st Timothy 5:22].

15. How does a man become a bishop?

The Pope chooses a priest who is known for his learning and holiness and appoints other bishops to consecrate him by imposing hands and praying to the Holy Spirit.

16. How does a man become Pope?

The Cardinals elect a new Pope after the death or resignation of his predecessor.

17. Why don't priests get married?

a) the consecrated single life helps them more easily to live a life of loving dedication to Jesus with an undivided heart [1st Corinthians 7:32-34];

b) thus they can more freely devote themselves to Him and through Him to the service of God and the care of God's people;

c) the single life lived for the sake of the kingdom of heaven is a witness and a sign to all of the values of that kingdom and the life to come.

18. Why is the priest called "Father"?

Because he gives the life of grace to his spiritual children, just as a father gives physical life to his children.

"I write these things not to put you to shame, but to admonish you as my dearest children. For although you have ten thousand tutors in Christ, yet you have not many fathers. For in Christ Jesus, through the gospel, did I beget you" [1st Corinthians 4:14-15].

THE POPE: the bishop of Rome, vicar of Christ on earth, successor of St. Peter, visible head of the whole Catholic Church.

CARDINAL: honorary title given to priests or bishops because of their important positions in the Church; they elect the new Pope.

BISHOP: the spiritual leader of a diocese; specially chosen and ordained as one of the successors of the Apostles; can ordain priests and other bishops.

MONSIGNOR: honorary title given to a priest by the Pope because of an important position in the Church or as a reward for faithful service.

PASTOR: the priest in charge of the administration of a parish.

PRIEST: diocesan priests work in a diocese; religious priests belong to a religious order, like the Franciscans, Dominicans, etc.

PERMANENT DEACON: a man, single or married, ordained by the bishop to work in parochial or diocesan ministry.

MONK: monks live in a monastery; follow a strict rule under a superior; like the Benedictines and the Trappists; some are priests, others are brothers.

BROTHER: a man dedicated to teaching, hospital work or contemplation; takes vows of poverty, chastity and obedience but does not receive the Sacrament of Holy Orders.

SISTER: a woman dedicated to teaching, hospital or social work, or contemplation; takes vows of poverty, chastity and obedience and belongs to a religious order or community.

Lesson 28: The Nature of Marriage

GOD MADE MARRIAGE

God created man in his image. In the image of God he created him. Male and female he created them. Then God blessed them and said to them, "Be fruitful and multiply; fill the earth and subdue it." [Genesis 1:27-28].

1. Who founded marriage?

God did, and He established the laws concerning marriage.

2. When did God put marriage into the plan for human living?

When He created Adam and Eve.

3. For what purposes did God found marriage?

a) the begetting and educating of children, and

b) the mutual help of husband and wife.

4. How do you know that God intended marriage for the begetting and education of children?

He said so - "Be fruitful and multiply" [Genesis 1:28]

"God Himself who said, 'It is not good for man to be alone' [Genesis 2:18] and 'who made man from the beginning male and female' [Matthew 19:4] wished to share with man a certain special participation in His own creative work." [Vatican Council II, The Church Today, par. 50].

5. Does not common sense show that marriage and married love are by nature designed for bringing children into the world?

Yes, the very evident differences between men and women show this.

A woman's body is made for the bearing and nursing of children. A man's body is stronger so that he can protect his family and give them food and shelter. Women tend to be kinder, more sympathetic, more emotional than men. These are the qualities especially needed in the motherly care and instruction of children.

6. How do you know that God intended marriage also for the mutual help and love of husband and wife?

Again, the Bible says so.

"Then the Lord God said, 'It is not good that man should be alone; I will make him a helper fit for him'" [Genesis 2:18].

"Let each one of you love his wife as himself, and let the wife see that she respects her husband." [Ephesians 5:33]

7. Does not common sense lead to this conclusion, too?

Yes, common sense shows that men and women are incomplete without one another but find their physical and spiritual completion in marriage.

A man needs the sympathy, understanding and encouragement of a wife, while the wife needs his love, affection and companionship.

8. What is the purpose of sex pleasure?

To attract husband and wife to that expression of mutual selfgiving which at the same time fosters and enriches their love for one another and makes them cooperators with God for the transmitting of human life.

9. Who are the only ones who may engage in the acts and pleasures of sex?

Only husband and wife who are validly married and acting according to God's holy plans and laws.

10. How many wives did God create for Adam?

Only one wife; God wanted this marriage to be the model for all marriages—one man and one woman.

"For this reason a man leaves his father and mother, and clings to his wife, and the two become one flesh" [Genesis 2:24].

11. How long did God want husband and wife to stay together?

Until death.

"A woman is bound as long as her husband is alive, but if her husband dies, she is free. Let her marry whom she pleases, only let it be in the Lord" [1st Corinthians 7:39].

12. Why did God want husband and wife to stay together until death?

One practical reason is that a mother cannot raise her children properly without a husband's help and support.

It takes 20 to 30 years to raise a family, a good part of the life span of a marriage. The law which requires their staying together until death is a great help for the stability of the home and family. Besides there is something about the nature of sacred married love which requires that the bond between husband and wife be unbreakable until death.

13. What is a valid marriage?

A true and real marriage that fulfills all the essential requirements of God and His Church.

No power on earth can break a valid Christian marriage that has been consummated. "What therefore God has joined together, let no man put asunder" [Mark 10:9].

14. What is an invalid marriage?

A union that is not a true marriage in the eyes of God.

A couple invalidly married must either separate or have the marriage made valid, if possible. "Neither fornicators . . . nor adulterers . . . will possess the kingdom of God" [1st Corinthians 6:9].

15. What is necessary for a valid marriage?

A single man and a single woman who are of age, free to marry and capable of sexual intercourse, who intend to live together and be faithful to each other until death, intend to raise a family and who are, in no other way, prohibited by the law of God from marrying.

For example, it is forbidden to marry close relatives, as uncles, aunts, nieces or nephews.

16. Did God make these laws only for Catholics?

No, all human beings have to obey these laws.

However, Catholics are aided also by Church laws which further protect the holiness of marriage. For example, a Catholic cannot marry validly except in the presence of a priest and two witnesses, except by special permission.

17. Does the state have authority to change God's laws?

No, because God made these laws long before there were any governments.

But, the State can make laws requiring a license and registration, and concerning health, property rights, and so on, as long as these laws are not against God's laws.

18. Can men and women find real happiness in marriage?

Yes, if they follow God's plan for marriage.

"Happy the husband of a good wife, twice lengthened are his days; a worthy wife brings joy to her husband and full is his life. A good wife is a generous gift bestowed upon him who fears the Lord; be he rich or poor, his heart is content, and a smile is ever on his face" [Sirach 26:1-4].

19. What is the greatest source of happiness in marriage?

Raising children in the fear and love of God.

Court records show fewer marriage breakups among couples with large families.

PRACTICAL POINTS

1. All laws, both human and divine, are made for the good of society. Once in a while, a law will work a hardship on an individual, and this is sometimes true of God's laws on marriage. But you marry for "better or for worse." So, if, through no fault of yours, your married life is unhappy or if your marriage has broken up, or if you find God's laws hard to observe, ask God for the strength to do His will; ask your crucified Saviour for the courage to carry your cross. The Sacrament of Matrimony gives married people special graces to live their lives according to God's laws. In any case, God made no exceptions to His laws on marriage; to break them for any reason is a serious sin.

2. Do not try to judge whether your marriage or anybody else's is valid or invalid. That can be done only by one who is skilled in the knowledge of these laws. The priest who is instructing you will tell you whether your marriage is valid or not.

Lesson 29: The Sins Against Marriage

SEPARATION AND REFUSING THE MARRIAGE DEBT

Yet, for fear of fornication, let each man have his own wife, and let each woman have her own husband. Let the husband render to the wife her due, and likewise the wife to the husband. The wife has not authority over her body, but the husband; the husband likewise has not authority over his body, but the wife. Do not deprive each other, except perhaps by consent, for a time, that you may give yourselves to prayer; and return together again lest Satan tempt you because you lack self-control. [1st Corinthians 7:2-6]

DIVORCE

And some of the Pharisees coming up asked him, testing him, "Is it lawful for a man to put away his wife?" But he answered and said to them, "What did Moses command you?" They said, "Moses permitted us to write a notice of dismissal, and to put her away." But Jesus said to them, "By reason of the hardness of your heart he wrote you that commandment. But from the beginning of creation God made them male and female. 'For this cause a man shall leave his father and mother, and cleave to his wife, and the two shall become one flesh.' Therefore now they are no longer two, but one flesh. What therefore, God has joined together, let no man put asunder." And in the house, his disciples again asked him concerning this. And he said to them, "Whoever puts away his wife and marries another, commits adultery against her; and if the wife puts aways her husband, and marries another, she commits adultery." [Mark 10:2-12]

1. **What are the sins against marriage?**

   a) Refusing the marriage debt

   b) Unlawful separation

   c) Divorce

   d) Sinful company keeping

   e) Adultery

   f) Artificial birth control

   g) Abortion

   h) Sterilization

2. What is the marriage debt?

The "marriage debt" means that a married person is obliged, under penalty of mortal sin, to give his (or her) married partner sexual intercourse whenever it is reasonably asked for.

Lawful excuses for refusing: adultery, sickness, drunkenness, insanity, non-support, danger to an unborn baby.

3. Should a married person always insist on the right to intercourse?

No, because a marriage cannot be successful unless it is founded on love and unselfishness.

4. Why is it a mortal sin to separate from your partner?

Separation in a *valid* marriage is a mortal sin because—

a) God said so.

b) To separate means to refuse the marriage debt (mortal sin).

c) A separated person is tempted to commit adultery or some other sin of sex.

d) Children cannot be properly trained.

5. Is a validly married person ever allowed to separate?

Yes, but only for a very serious reason. Except in extraordinary cases, such as immediate threat of physical harm, no one should make a decision about separation without consultation with one's pastor or confessor.

6. Why is divorce and remarriage a mortal sin?

Because it is clearly against the law of God.

"Everyone who puts away his wife and marries another commits adultery; and he who marries a woman who has been put away from her husband commits adultery" [Luke 16:18].

"A woman is bound as long as her husband is alive, but if her husband dies, she is free. Let her marry whom she pleases" [1st Corinthians 7:39].

7. May a separated or divorced person keep company with another?

No, not if the marriage is valid, because such a person is still married, and a married person is never allowed to keep company with another.

"Therefore while her husband is alive, she will be called an adulteress if she be with another man" [Romans 7:3].

8. What is adultery?

Sexual intercourse which a married person has with someone to whom he (or she) is not married. If both adulterers are married, the act is doubly sinful.

9. What is artificial (contraceptive) birth control?

Doing anything before, during or after intercourse to keep a woman from becoming pregnant.

10. Is artificial birth control allowed?

No. "Each and every marriage act (intercourse) must remain open to the transmission of life" [Pope Paul VI, *On the Regulation of Birth*]

"Similarly excluded (i.e. morally forbidden) is every action which, either in anticipation of the conjugal act, or in its accomplishment, or in the development of its natural consequences, proposes ... to render procreation impossible." [Pope Paul VI].

11. What is the sin of abortion?

Killing an unborn baby.

12. Is abortion ever allowed to save a mother's life?

No, because directly attacking the life of an innocent human being, including that of an unborn baby, is always murder.

13. What happens to a Catholic who knowingly and directly cooperates in procuring an abortion?

Automatic excommunication is the penalty for this crime.

This means that such a person is excluded from receiving the Sacraments.

14. Can an excommunicated person get back into the church?

Yes, if with true repentance he confesses the crime.

However, the priest who hears his confession has to get special power from the bishop to take away the excommunication.

15. What is sterilization?

Making the reproductive organs unfruitful, usually by tying or cutting the Fallopian tubes or seminal vesicles, or by removing the womb or ovaries.

16. What kind of sin is sterilization?

Always a mortal sin, unless the organs are diseased and are a danger to the health of the whole body.

PRACTICAL POINTS

1. The sins discussed in this lesson are against the law of God and are, therefore, forbidden to everyone, not just Catholics.

2. If lack of money or poor health make it difficult for you to have children, consider that this is the cross Jesus wants you to carry and that He will give you the strength to carry it.

3. If there are serious reasons to postpone a pregnancy or to space out births, reasons which come from the physical or psychological conditions of husband and wife or from external conditions, the Church teaches that it is then lawful to take into account the natural rhythms of the mother's generative system and to restrict the use of marriage to the infertile periods only. This manner of regulating births does not offend the moral principles which prohibit artificial contraception.

4. In dealing with doctors, women should cautiously regard any suggestions concerning emptying the uterus, terminating the pregnancy, tying the tubes. Such expressions are medical jargon for procedures which have great moral implications.

Lesson 30: The Sacrament of Matrimony

Be subject to one another in the fear of Christ. Let wives be subject to their husbands as to the Lord; because a husband is head of the wife, just as Christ is head of the Church, being himself saviour of the body. But just as the Church is subject to Christ, so also let wives be to their husbands in all things.

Husbands, love your wives, just as Christ also loved the Church, and delivered himself up for her, that he might sanctify her, cleansing her in the bath of water by means of the word; in order that he might present to himself the Church in all her glory, not having spot or wrinkle or any such thing, but that she might be holy and without blemish. Even thus ought husbands also to love their wives as their own bodies. He who loves his own wife, loves himself. For no one ever hated his own flesh; on the contrary he nourishes and cherishes it, as Christ also does the Church [because we are members of his body, made from his flesh and from his bones]. "For this cause a man shall leave his father and mother, and cleave to his wife; and the two shall become one flesh." This is a great mystery—I mean in reference to Christ and to the Church.

However, let each one of you also love his wife just as he loves himself; and let the wife respect her husband. [Ephesians 5:21-33]

1. What is the Sacrament of Matrimony?

Matrimony is the Sacrament made by Jesus Christ to sanctify (make holy) the lawful union of a Christian man and woman.

2. Was marriage always a Sacrament?

No, marriage, although always a sacred union of man and woman, was raised to the dignity of a Sacrament by Jesus Christ.

3. What does this Sacrament do for a couple?

a) It gives an increase of that grace which is a share in God's own life;

b) it gives them special helps to perform their duties as married people and to overcome the difficulties that may come into their married life.

4. Who may receive the Sacrament of Matrimony?

Only those who have been baptized and are free to marry.

5. What is necessary to receive this Sacrament worthily?

You have to be free of mortal sin.

6. What kind of sin is it to receive this Sacrament unworthily?

A mortal sin of sacrilege.

However, the marriage is valid.

7. Do Catholics have to be married at Mass?

No, but it is certainly fitting that they do so.

The special Mass for a Catholic wedding is called Nuptial Mass. Permission may be obtained for marriage at Holy Mass in the case of a mixed marriage.

8. What should a Catholic do who wants to marry?

Preparations for the wedding should be made at least one month in advance with one of the priests in the parish of the bride, or in the parish of the Catholic party in the case of a mixed marriage.

9. Are the marriages of non-Catholics valid?

Yes, provided all the laws of God concerning marriage are observed, the marriages of non-Catholics among themselves are valid and, therefore, cannot be broken.

Non-Catholic can marry validly in the presence of anyone who can perform marriages legally [minister, rabbi, judge, justice of the peace, captain of a ship].

PRACTICAL POINTS

1. It is not the priest who is the minister of the Sacrament of Matrimony; he is only the chief witness. The bride and groom are the ministers of this Sacrament. They administer it to each other when they exchange their marriage consent. The first gift they give one another, therefore, is God's life-grace. It is fitting indeed that this giving should be done at Holy Mass.

2. "Christian spouses have a special sacrament by which they are fortified and receive a kind of consecration in the duties and dignity of their state. By virtue of this sacrament, as spouses fulfill their conjugal and family obligations ... they increasingly advance toward their own perfection as well as their mutual sanctification, and hence contribute jointly to the glory of God. As a result, with their parents leading the way by example and family prayer, children and indeed everyone gathered around the family hearth will more easily find the path to human maturity, salvation and holiness." (Vatican Council II, *The Church Today,* par. 48)

NOTES

Lesson 31: **How to Have a Happy Marriage**

Then Tobias exhorted the virgin, and said to her: "Sara, arise, and let us pray to God today, and tomorrow, and the next day, because for these three nights we are joined to God. And when the third night is over, we will be in our own wedlock. For we are the children of saints, and we must not be joined together like heavens that know not God." So they both arose and prayed earnestly both together that health might be given them. And Tobias said: "Lord God of our fathers, may the heavens and the earth, and the sea, and the fountains, and the rivers, and all thy creatures that are in them, bless thee. Thou madest Adam of the slime of the earth, and gave him Eve for a helper. And now, Lord, thou knowest, that not for fleshly lust do I take my sister to wife, but only for the love of posterity, in which thy name may be blessed forever and ever." Sara also said: "Have mercy on us, O Lord, have mercy on us: and let us grow old both together in health." [Tobias 8:4-10]

1. Have the correct attitude.

Look upon marriage as a very holy union, founded by God and raised to the dignity of a Sacrament by Jesus Christ as a means to holiness and eternal salvation.

2. Have the correct purpose.

Look forward to having children and founding a Christian home.

> *People who marry for selfish reasons (money, pleasure, beauty, fame, influence) very seldom, if ever, find happiness in marriage.*

3. Don't marry for selfish reasons.

Genuine happiness is attained only by those who are completely generous and ready to sacrifice themselves in all things.

4. Study to understand better what marriage is.

Marriage, like other vocations, requires special knowledge obtained through study and prayer.

> *Attend a Pre-Cana Conference or a Catholic marriage forum, or at least receive marriage instructions from your parish priest.*

5. Pray for a holy and happy marriage.

You should pray every day for a holy and happy marriage, because your final judgment before God will certainly deal with how you have lived your married life, your vocation from God.

> *"Home and possessions are an inheritance from parents, but a prudent wife is from the Lord"* [Proverbs 19:14].

6. Prepare for marriage by living a good Catholic life.

Go to Holy Mass and Holy Communion very often; receive the Sacrament of Penance regularly; obey the Ten Commandments, especially the 6th and 9th and live by the Sermon on the Mount.

7. Follow the advice of your parents and your parish priest.

It is wise to seek advice when making any important decision, but especially when deciding about a life-long union.

8. Choose a good partner.

Look for someone who shares your Catholic ideals and who is really serious about founding a good family and a Christian home, a person who is sincere, truthful, dependable, and chaste.

9. Don't marry too young.

Today young men and women under twenty-one, though capable of having children, are very frequently immature and undeveloped mentally and emotionally, so that they do not understand the dignity, beauty and seriousness of marriage.

10. Have the right attitude toward sex.

God created sex and sex pleasure to attract husband and wife to that expression of mutual self-giving, which at the same time fosters and enriches their love for one another, and makes them cooperators with Him for the transmitting of human life.

11. Have a gallant and generous attitude toward the vocation and challenge of Christian parenthood.

Look upon having children as one of the great blessings of marriage.

> *"Children are really the supreme gift of marriage"* [Vatican Council II, The Church Today, par. 50]

12. Have respect for your partner.

The person you marry shares in a union that was established by God Himself and raised to the dignity of a Sacrament by Christ.

"Husbands, in like manner dwell with your wives considerately, paying honor to the woman as to the weaker vessel, and as co-heir of the grace of life, that your prayers be not hindered" [1st Peter 3:7].

13. Don't fight or argue!

Married people should learn to control their tempers and to discuss their problems as grown-ups and not as children.

"Bear with one another and forgive one another, if anyone has a grievance against any other; even as the Lord has forgiven you, so also do you forgive. But above all these things have charity, which is the bond of perfection. And may the peace of Christ reign in your hearts; unto that peace, indeed, you were called in one body ... Wives be subject to your husbands, as is becoming in the Lord. Husbands, love your wives and do not be bitter toward them" [Colossians 3:13-15, 18-19].

14. Don't criticize!

Criticizing your partner's faults or constantly harping on trifles soon destroys a happy marriage.

"But why dost thou seek the speck in thy brother's eye, and yet dost not consider the beam in thy own eye? Or how canst thou say to thy brother, 'Let me cast out the speck from thy eye'; and behold, there is a beam in thy own eye?" [Matthew 7:3-4].

15. Trust one another completely.

It is a sin to be jealous or judge without evidence.

"Do not judge, that you may not be judged. For with what judgment you judge, you shall be judged; and with what measure you measure, it shall be measured to you" [Matthew 7:1].

16. Don't live with in-laws!

Your first duty is to your married partner; parents and others come second.

"For this reason a man leaves his father and mother, and clings to his wife, and the two become one flesh" [Genesis 2:24].

17. Do things together.

Husband and wife should find happiness in their own home with their children, and also should associate with other happily married couples.

18. Make your home a pleasant place.

The wife should make the home a place to which her husband longs to go after his day's work; it should be clean and orderly, and the meals well prepared.

"Happy the husband of a good wife, twice lenghened are his days; a worthy wife brings joy to her husband, peaceful and full is his life. A good wife is a generous gift bestowed upon him who fears the Lord; be he rich or poor, his heart is content, and a smile is ever on his face" [Sirach 26:1-4].

19. Use family money properly.

A husband is bound to complete support of his wife and children; a wife is obliged to use the family money wisely.

"If anyone does not take care of his own, and especially of his household, he has denied the faith and is worse than an unbeliever" [1st Timothy 5.8].

20. Pray together!

As the saying goes, "The family that prays together stays together" and this includes attending Mass and receiving Holy Communion together.

"Where two or three are gathered together for my sake, there am I in the midst of them" [Matthew 18:20].

NOTES

Lesson 32:

Duties of Parents Toward Their Children

Whoever causes one of these little ones who believe in me to sin, it would be better for him to have a great millstone hung around his neck, and to be drowned in the depths of the sea. [Matthew 18:6]

1. To give their children the necessary food, clothing and shelter.

This obligation rests on *both* parents, whether living together or separated. They must also keep their children from all danger to life or health.

2. To give good example.

Parents give good example by faithfully observing all their religious duties of attending Holy Mass, observing religious practices of penance on Fridays and during Lent, by fostering prayer, decent speech, respect for God's holy name, honesty, chastity, merciful love of neighbor, sobriety.

Parents should remember that children are great imitators, and should be very careful of everything they do and say in the presence of their children.

3. To provide a truly Christian home for them.

A Christian Home is one in which God and Religion are of the greatest importance.

In the home there should be a crucifix, pictures of Jesus, the Blessed Virgin and of the Saints. Indecent pictures and calendars, sexy and sensational magazines, books and comic books, have no place in the Christian home.

4. To have them baptized as soon as possible after birth.

It is a serious sin to delay the Baptism of infants, and if there is any danger to the life of the newly born baby, the priest should be called immediately.

5. To see that they receive Holy Communion, go to Confession and receive Confirmation.

The children should be taught to go to Holy Communion and Confession regularly and frequently, every week, if possible, especially during vacation time.

6. To teach them to pray.

Daily prayers should be said by the whole family together.

As the saying goes, "A family that prays together stays together."

7. To see that they attend Mass every Sunday and on the six Holy Days.

Parents should not keep children home from Mass except for very serious reasons.

8. To give them the Christian attitude on marriage and having children.

Parents should avoid complaining about the hardships of married life and joking about the sacred duties of marriage.

The birth of another child should be a joyful occasion for the whole family so that the other children will consider having children as the greatest blessing of married life.

9. To prepare them for marriage.

The children should be taught the serious duties and responsibilities of marriage both by word and example.

They should also be taught the practical side of making a home, such as cleaning, cooking, sewing, repairing, being on time, neatness and orderliness.

10. To give them right knowledge and right attitudes about human sexuality.

This information should be given carefully and with great emphasis on the beauty and sacredness of sex.

Answers to questions about the facts of life should be correct but always suited to the age and mental development of the child. Parents should encourage the confidence of their children so that the children will go to them for information.

11. To correct their sins and faults.

It is a serious sin to neglect this duty.

12. To teach them the virtues of honesty, obedience, truthfulness and purity.

These lessons must be given early and constantly.

13. To teach them respect for the rights and property of others.

Many parents sin seriously by bad example in this matter.

14. To teach them respect for all lawful authority.

Children should be taught early to respect all lawful authority especially the authority of the Church, the State and the School.

15. To give them wholesome recreation and keep them from evil companions.

The Christian Home should be the center of the child's social life, a place where he feels free to bring his companions.

Parents should consult the moral rating list before allowing their children to attend a motion picture, check their reading matter, and govern their use of the radio and television. Children receive many false ideas on life, marriage, crime, drinking and so on, from these sources of entertainment.

16. To encourage a child's desire to be a priest, religious brother or sister or consecrated lay missionary.

Having a person in the family called to such a beautiful vocation is one of the greatest blessings that God can give a mother and father. Parents should encourage children who give signs of such a calling.

THE TEN COMMANDMENTS

1st. I am the Lord thy God. Thou shalt not have strange gods before Me.
2nd. Thou shalt not take the name of the Lord thy God in vain.
3rd. Remember thou keep holy the Sabbath Day.
4th. Honor thy father and thy mother.
5th. Thou shalt not kill.
6th. Thou shalt not commit adultery.
7th. Thou shalt not steal.
8th. Thou shalt not bear false witness against thy neighbor.
9th. Thou shalt not covet thy neighbor's wife.
10th. Thou shalt not covet thy neighbor's goods.

In studying the Ten Commandments, keep in mind the reason why God created you—to share in His happiness in heaven. God gave the Ten Commandments, not to make life difficult for you, but to help you get to heaven. "If thou wilt enter into life, keep the commandments" [Matthew 19:17]. The Ten Commandments are another indication of God's great love for you.

Lesson 33: The First Commandment

Come, let us sing joyfully to the Lord; let us acclaim the Rock of our salvation. Let us greet him with thanksgiving; let us joyfully sing psalms to him. For the Lord is a great God, and a great king above all gods; in his hands are the depths of the earth, and the tops of the mountains are his. His is the sea, for he has made it, and the dry land, which his hands have formed. Come, let us bow down in worship; let us kneel before the Lord who made us. For he is our God, and we are the people he shepherds, the flock he guides. [Psalm 95:1-7]

1. What is the First Commandment?

I am the Lord thy God; thou shalt not have strange gods before Me.

2. What does the First Commandment oblige you to do?

To offer true worship to God.

"Worship him who made the heaven and the earth, the sea and fountains of waters" [Apocalypse (Revelations) 14:7].

3. What is worship?

Acknowledging the fact that God created you and that you depend entirely on Him.

"For in him we live and move and have our being" [Acts 17:28].

4. How do you worship God?

By praying to Him both in private and in public.

"And they were continually in the temple, praising and blessing God" [Luke 24:53].

5. Is there a special name for public worship in our Lord's Church?

Yes, liturgical worship or the Liturgy of the Church.

6. Is liturgy important in the life of the Church?

a) It is the high point, the highest action, toward which all the other activity of the Church is directed; it is the fountain from which all her power flows;

b) Actively taking part in liturgical worship is the necessary and first source from which faithful Catholics are to derive the true Christian spirit.

The liturgy consists mainly in Holy Mass, the Sacraments, the Divine Office, the observance of the feasts of the Church Year.

7. How do many people sin against the First Commandment?

By negligence in their duty to give worship to God.

8. Why is it a sin to believe in fortune telling?

Because to do so is to attribute to a creature knowledge that belongs only to God.

Only God knows the future and He certainly does not reveal it in silly ways, through such things as tea leaves, bumps on your head, lines on your palm, movements of the stars and planets.

9. Why is it a sin to guide your life by dreams?

a) God forbids it many times in the Bible.

b) It is foolish and may lead to other sins.

"Unless it be a vision specially sent by the Most High, fix not your heart on it; for dreams have led many astray, and those who believed in them have perished" [Sirach 34:6-7].

NOTES

_____

_____

_____

_____

_____

_____

_____

_____

Lesson 34: **The Second Commandment**

Let the kings of the earth and all peoples, the princes and all the judges of the earth, young men too, and maidens, old men and boys, praise the name of the Lord, for his name alone is exalted. [Psalm 148:11-13]

And appearing in the form of man, he humbled himself, becoming obedient to death, even to death on the cross. Therefore God also has exalted him and has bestowed upon him the name that is above every name, so that at the name of Jesus every knee should bend of those in heaven, on earth and under the earth, and every tongue should confess that the Lord Jesus Christ is in the glory of God the Father. [Philippians 2:7-11]

1. What is the Second Commandment?

Thou shalt not take the name of the Lord, your God in vain.

"For the Lord will not leave unpunished him who takes his name in vain" [Exodus 20:7].

2. What does the Second Commandment oblige you to do?

Always to use the Name of God and of Jesus Christ reverently.

"Holy is his name" [Luke 1:49].

3. What are the sins against the Second Commandment?

a) Misusing the Name of God or of Jesus Christ,

b) blasphemy,

c) breaking an oath.

4. How may you misuse the name of God?

By using it without good reason and without respect.

This is generally a venial sin.

5. What is blasphemy?

An expression insulting to God or religion.

It is a mortal sin when the blasphemer really intends to insult God.

6. What kind of sin is it to use vulgar language?

To say "hell" or "damn" or to use other vulgar language is not a sin.

Of course, it would be sinful if in using the word "damn" you really intended that some person be sent to hell. Also, there can be sins of anger or impatience when using this kind of vulgar language.

"Out of the same mouth proceed blessing and cursing. These things, my brethren, ought not to be so" [James 3:10].

7. What is an oath?

Calling on God to be witness to the truth.

8. What kind of sin is it to break an oath?

A mortal sin, called perjury.

It is mortal, even in a small matter, because an oath calls upon God to witness the lie.

9. What is a vow?

A special promise made to God by which a person freely assumes an obligation binding under penalty of sin to do something especially pleasing to God.

The vows of poverty, chastity and obedience which are taken by persons who belong to religious orders in the Church are promises to live a life of Gospel poverty, a consecrated single life, and a life of generous obedience to their religious superiors.

NOTES

Lesson 35: The Third Commandment

Remember to keep holy the Sabbath day. Six days you may labor and do all your work, but the seventh day is the Sabbath of the Lord, your God. No work may be done then either by you, or your son or daughter, or your male or female slave, or your beast, or by the alien who lives with you. In six days the Lord made the heavens and the earth, the sea and all that is in them; but on the seventh day he rested. That is why the Lord has blessed the Sabbath day and made it holy. [Exodus 20:8-11]

1. What is the Third Commandment?

Remember thou keep holy the Sabbath Day.

2. What does the Third Commandment oblige you to do?

For Catholics this means observing Sunday as a day of rest and participating in Holy Mass. In many places, the Mass obligation can be fulfilled on Saturday evening.

3. What are the six Holy Days of Obligation (obligatory attendance at Mass) in the United States?

1) Christmas - Dec. 25.

2) Solemnity of Mary the Mother of God - Jan. 1.

3) Ascension Thursday - 40 days after Easter.

4) Assumption of the Blessed Virgin Mary - Aug. 15.

5) Solemnity of All Saints - Nov. 1.

6) Immaculate Conception of Mary - Dec. 8.

4. Is the duty of attending Mass on Sundays and Holy Days a serious obligation?

It is, and therefore to miss Mass through your own fault is a serious sin.

5. Are you ever excused from the obligation of hearing Mass?

Yes, but only for a serious reason.

Examples: sickness, caring for a sick person, long distance from the church, necessary work.

6. Can a priest excuse you from the obligation?

Yes, your pastor, or the priest in Confession, can excuse you for a sufficient reason.

7. What does the Third Commandment oblige you as a parent?

You have the serious obligation to see that your children attend Mass on Sundays and Holy Days.

8. What does it mean to say that Sundays must be observed as days of rest?

Manual (heavy) work is forbidden, unless it is truly necessary.

Acts of charity such as taking care of the sick and ordinary necessary household chores are, of course, permitted. Some works done as a hobby such as light gardening would be all right, but such things as overhauling an auto or doing the weekly laundry compromise the spirit of Sunday holiness and rest.

9. Is it wrong to engage in sports and other recreation on Sunday?

No, unless they interfere with your religious obligations.

Examples: playing games, dancing, movies.

NOTE

1. The Church changed the Lord's Day from Saturday to Sunday because our Lord rose from the dead on Sunday and the Holy Spirit came down upon the Apostles on Pentecost Sunday.

2. "The Lord's day is the original feast day, and it should be proposed to the piety of the faithful and taught to them in such a way that it may become in fact a day of joy and of freedom from work ... the foundation and nucleus of the whole liturgical year." [Vatican Council II, *Liturgy,* par. 106]

Lesson 36: **The Fourth Commandment**

My son, take care of your father when he is old; grieve him not as long as he lives. Even if his mind fail, be considerate with him; revile him not in the fullness of your strength. For kindness to a father will not be forgotten, it will serve as a sin offering — it will take lasting root. In time of tribulation it will be recalled to your advantage, like warmth upon frost, it will melt away your sins. [Sirach 3:12-15]

1. What is the Fourth Commandment?

Honor thy father and thy mother.

"With your whole heart honor your father; your mother's birthpangs forget not. Remember, of these parents you were born; what can you give them for all they gave you?" [Sirach 3:1-15].

2. What are the duties of children toward their parents?

a) To love and respect them as long as they live;

b) to obey them in all things, except sin;

c) to help them in their old age, or when they are sick and helpless;

d) to see that they receive the Last Sacraments and a Catholic funeral.

3. How long is a child obliged to obey his parents?

Until the 21st birthday, or until he or she leaves home, for example, to marry or to become a priest or sister.

4. Do your parents come before your married partner?

No, your first obligation is to your married partner and your children.

5. What are the sins against the Fourth Commandment?

Disobeying one's parents, hating, threatening, cursing, striking, insulting them, being ashamed of them, wishing them evil, speaking or acting unkindly toward them, causing them anger or sorrow.

6. What else does the Fourth Commandment oblige you to do?

To respect all lawful authority, especially the authority of the Church and the State.

> *"Let everyone be subject to the higher authorities, for there exists no authority except from God, and those who exist have been appointed by God. Therefore he who resists the authority resists the ordinance of God ... Render to all men whatever is their due; tribute to whom tribute is due; taxes to whom taxes are due; fear to whom fear is due; honor to whom honor is due"* [Romans 13:17].

7. What are the duties of parents toward their children?

See Lesson 32, Page 106.

PRACTICAL POINTS

1. Patriotism is a Christian virtue and a Christian duty. It involves love of one's country, interest in its welfare, respect and obedience toward civil authority. Honest and responsible voting in elections, paying just taxes, defending our country's rights are moral obligations.

2. If the government passes laws that violate the law of God, we must oppose those laws and even refuse to obey them. "We must obey God rather than men" [Acts 5:29]

NOTES

_____

_____

_____

_____

_____

_____

_____

Lesson 37: The Fifth Commandment

Then the Lord God formed man out of the dust of the ground and breathed into his nostrils the breath of life, and man became a living being. [Genesis 2:7]

1. What is the Fifth Commandment?

Thou shalt not kill.

2. What does the Fifth Commandment oblige you to do?

To safeguard the life and health and physical welfare of ourselves and others.

3. What are the mortal sins against the Fifth Commandment?

a) Murder, the unjust killing of an innocent person.

b) Abortion, deliberately causing the death of an unborn baby.

c) Suicide, taking your own life.

d) "Mercy killing," killing an innocent person who is dying of an incurable disease.

e) Causing serious injury or death by criminal neglect.

f) Sterilization, making the sex organs unfruitful.

g) Getting seriously drunk.

h) Serious anger and hatred.

4. Are you ever allowed to use force or to kill?

Only in self-defense, when it is the only way you can protect life and when your life is being seriously attacked here and now.

5. Is abortion ever allowed?

No, because deliberately and directly causing the death of an innocent person, including that of an unborn baby, is murder.

> *Catholics who cooperate in procuring an abortion are automatically excommunicated from the Church. See the lesson on sins against marriage.*

6. Is suicide ever allowed?

No, your life belongs to God, and He alone can take it away.

A Catholic who commits suicide while in his right mind loses his right to have a Catholic funeral.

7. Is "mercy killing" ever allowed?

No, because it is murder.

A person who allows himself to be killed in this way is guilty of suicide.

8. Is sterilization ever allowed?

To have the Fallopian tubes or the seminal vesicles tied or cut is a form of mutilation and is a mortal sin.

Reproductive organs may be surgically removed or rendered inoperative only when they are themselves diseased or associated with some disease that presents a danger to the whole body. Sterilization as a contraceptive measure is immoral.

9. What kind of sin is it to get drunk?

Complete intoxication, serious drunkenness, is a mortal sin; overdrinking short of this excess is a venial sin.

Habitual drinking that seriously injures one's health or gives scandal or destroys a person's sense of duty to provide for his family is a mortal sin even if the drinker never becomes seriously drunk.

10. Are you ever allowed to use narcotics?

Only when recommended by a competent doctor, and then only according to his directions.

11. Are hatred and anger mortal sins?

They are usually venial unless you wish someone serious harm.

12. Is there such a thing as sinless anger?

Yes, anger prompted by zeal for justice, honor to God, or some other good cause.

Jesus, for example, was angry with the buyers and sellers in the temple.

13. In a war of defense against unjust aggression, may we use any and all means to oppose the enemy?

We may not engage in acts of war or use weapons that attack innocent and helpless citizens of the enemy country. The idea of "total war" must be condemned.

"Any act of war aimed indiscriminately at the destruction of entire cities or of extensive areas along with their population is a crime against God and man himself. It merits unequivocal and unhesitating condemnation." [Vatican Council II, The Church Today, par. 80]

PRACTICAL POINTS

1. The word "obscene" which used to refer to matters offensive to chastity is now often used to describe the scenes of offensive physical violence in so many modern movies and television programs. Constantly watching programs depicting so much fighting, anger, hatred and revenge along with the bodily injury and suffering that results from such vicious sentiments hardly disposes a person to think in times of conflict of the admonitions of Jesus: "Blessed are the meek ... Blessed are the peacemakers ... Forgive seventy times seven."

2. "Those who are pledged to the service of their country as members of its armed forces should regard themselves as agents of security and freedom on behalf of their people. As long as they fulfill this role properly, they are making a genuine contribution to the establishment of peace." [Vatican Council II, *The Church Today,* par. 79]

NOTES

Lesson 38: The Sixth and Ninth Commandments

Now the body is not for immorality, but for the Lord, and the Lord for the body. Now God has raised up the Lord and will also raise us up by his power. Do you not know that your bodies are members of Christ? Shall I then take the members of Christ and make them members of a harlot? By no means! Or do you not know that he who cleaves to a harlot, becomes one body with her? "For the two," it says, "shall be one flesh." But he who cleaves to the Lord is one spirit with him. Flee immorality. Every sin that man commits is outside the body, but the immoral man sins against his own body. Or do you not know that your members are the temple of the Holy Spirit, who is in you, whom you have from God, and that you are not your own? For you have been bought at a great price. Glorify God and bear him in your body. [1st Corinthians 6:13-20]

1. What is the Sixth Commandment?

Thou shalt not commit adultery.

2. What is the Ninth Commandment?

Thou shalt not covet thy neighbor's wife.

3. What do these commandments oblige you to do?

To practice the virtue of chastity according to your state in life.

Chastity regulates the use of sex for married people. Chastity forbids the use of sex to unmarried people.

4. Who are the only ones who may engage in the acts and pleasures of sex?

Only husband and wife who are validly married and are acting according to God's holy plans and laws.

5. Name some of the sins against the Sixth Commandment.

a) Adultery

b) Fornication

c) Self-abuse

d) Impure touches, looks, kisses, dancing, reading

e) Looking at impure pictures, dances, floor shows, movies

f) Sins against nature

g) Indecent dressing

6. What is adultery?

Sexual intercourse which a married person has with someone to whom he (or she) is not married.

"For God will judge the immoral and adulterers" [Hebrews 13:4].

7. What is fornication?

Sexual intercourse between an unmarried man and an unmarried woman.

8. What is self-abuse?

Enjoying the sexual pleasure alone; also called masturbation.

9. What are sins against nature?

Perversions committed with another person or with animals.

"Do not err; neither fornicators, nor idolators, nor adulterers, nor the effeminate, nor sodomites ... will possess the kingdom of God" [1st Corinthians 6:9-10].

10. What is forbidden by the Ninth Commandment?

Impure thoughts and desires.

"But I say to you that anyone who so much as looks with lust at a woman has already committed adultery with her in his heart" [Matthew 5:28].

11. When do you become guilty of impure thoughts?

When you knowingly and willingly keep such thoughts in your mind.

"For from within, out of the heart of men, come evil thoughts, adulteries, immorality" [Mark 7:21].

12. Is it possible to lead a pure life?

Yes, with God's help—

a) if you stay away from near occasions of sin, that is, all persons, places and things which easily lead into sin;

b) if you pray often and receive the Sacraments of Penance and Holy Eucharist regularly and often;

c) if you avoid idleness;

d) if you practice self-denial even in good things, for example, giving up in a spirit of Christian sacrifice some good things which you like, doing some good things which you don't like.

"And everyone in a contest abstains from all things—and they indeed to receive a perishable crown, but we an imperishable" [1st Corinthians 9:25].

NOTE

"In the area of sexuality, the Christian is to be modest in behavior and dress. In a sex-saturated society, the follower of Christ must be different. For the Christian there can be no premarital sex, fornication, adultery, or other acts of impurity or scandal to others. He must remain chaste, repelling lustful desires and temptations, self-abuse, pornography and indecent entertainment of every description." [*Basic Teachings,* American Bishops, par. 19]

NOTES

Lesson 39:

The Seventh and Tenth Commandments

God created man in his image. In the image of God he created him. Male and female he created them. Then God blessed them and said to them, "Be fruitful and multiply; fill the earth and subdue it. Have dominion over the fish of the sea, the birds of the air, the cattle and all the animals that crawl on earth." God also said, "See, I give you every seed-bearing plant on the earth and every tree which has seed-bearing fruit to be your food." [Genesis 1:27-29]

1. What is the Seventh Commandment?

Thou shalt not steal.

2. What is the Tenth Commandment?

Thou shalt not covet thy neighbor's goods.

3. What do these commandments oblige you to do?

To respect the property of others.

4. What is meant by stealing?

Taking anything which does not belong to you and which the owner is not willing to give you.

5. What does stealing include?

a) Robbery and burglary.

b) Graft and bribes.

c) Cheating and fraud.

d) Not paying bills, taxes and debts.

e) Not supporting your family.

f) Damaging the property of others.

g) Wasting time or materials on your job.

h) Not giving employees a just wage.

6. What kind of sin is it to steal?

Stealing something expensive is a mortal sin; stealing something cheap is a venial sin.

7. Are you ever allowed to keep stolen goods?

No, you have to give the goods back to the person from whom they were stolen, whether you stole them yourself or got them from somebody else.

No matter how small the theft—silverware, ash trays, towels—you must give it back.

8. What must you do if you can't find the owner?

Give the stolen goods to charity.

9. What must you do if you damage someone's property?

You must pay for the damage, or else be guilty of sin.

The sin is mortal or venial depending on the value of the object damaged or destroyed.

10. What should you do with something you find?

Try to find the owner.

If the article is expensive, then you must spend some money advertising for him. He has to pay you the money you spent in trying to find him.

11. Is gambling a sin?

It is no sin to gamble if—

a) it is your money;

b) you do not deprive your family of the things they need;

c) everyone has an equal chance to win.

12. What are the duties of employees?

a) Not to waste time or materials.

b) To do the job as well as possible.

c) To respect the terms of labor-management contracts that are the result of just collective bargaining.

d) To respect the rights of employers and conscientiously to defend the rights of fellow workers, for example, by encouraging good and honest labor unions.

13. What are the duties of employers?

a) To pay their employees a just wage.

b) To provide for the safety of all employees.

c) To respect the terms of labor-management contracts that are the result of just collective bargaining.

d) To use only honest means to defend their own rights while respecting the rights of their workers, for example, the right to form honest labor unions.

NOTES

_____

_____

_____

_____

_____

_____

_____

_____

_____

_____

_____

_____

_____

_____

_____

_____

_____

_____

Lesson 40: **The Eighth Commandment**

The tongue is placed among our members, defiling the whole body, and setting on fire the course of our life, being itself set on fire by hell. For every kind of beast and bird, and of serpents and the rest, is tamed and has been tamed by mankind; but the tongue no man can tame—a restless evil, full of deadly poison. With it we bless God the Father; and with it we curse men, who have been made after the likeness of God. Out of the same mouth proceed blessing and cursing. These things, my brethren, ought not to be. [James 3:6-10]

1. What is the Eighth Commandment?

Thou shalt not bear false witness against thy neighbor.

2. What does the Eighth Commandment oblige you to do?

To use the power of speech according to God's plan, that is, always to tell the truth.

3. Name some of the sins against the Eighth Commandment.

a) Lying

b) Hurting someone's reputation

c) Unjust criticism

d) Gossip

e) Insults

f) Not keeping secrets

g) Judging another without evidence

h) Making known the sins of others

i) Perjury

4. What kind of sin is it to tell a lie?

Mortal sin, if it harms someone seriously; otherwise, it is venial.

5. Are you ever allowed to tell a lie?

No, not even a small one, not even to save someone's life or reputation.

"Wherefore, put away lying and speak truth each one with his neighbor, because we are members of one another" [Ephesians 4:25].

6. What must you do if you have told lies about another?

You have to do everything you can to restore his good name and make up any losses he suffered because of your lies.

7. Is it a sin to make known the hidden sins of another?

Yes, unless someone else would suffer harm; in such a case you are obliged to tell the proper authorities.

8. Is it a sin to listen to gossip?

Yes, because you are cooperating in another's sin.

It is a duty of charity to defend the reputation of another when it is being attacked.

9. Is perjury a sin?

Telling a lie after swearing to God to tell the truth is always a mortal sin.

"The false witness will not go unpunished, and he who utters lies will perish" [Proverbs 19:9].

10. Are you morally obliged to keep a secret?

Yes, if your revealing the secret would injure someone's right to privacy or secrecy.

For example: if you have given your promise to keep the secret; if your position is such, counselor, doctor, lawyer, that clients have a right to presume professional secrecy.

Lesson 41: Faith, Hope, Love

"Therefore, since we are justified by FAITH, we have peace with God through our Lord Jesus Christ. Through Him we have obtained access to this grace in which we stand, and we rejoice in our HOPE of sharing the glory of God. And hope does not disappoint us, because God's LOVE has been poured into our hearts through the Holy Spirit which has been given to us." [Romans 5:1-2, 5]

1. What duties does the virtue of faith help you fulfill?

The duty to believe firmly all that God has revealed, to defend your Catholic faith openly when necessary, to fight temptations against faith, to witness your faith to others with a real missionary zeal.

2. What duties does the virtue of hope help you fulfill?

The duty to trust firmly that God will give you eternal salvation and all the means to obtain it, to fight temptations against Christian hope.

Sins against hope: giving up hope and trust in God (despair); hoping in the wrong way, for example, by trusting in God's mercy while refusing to repent of your sins or to amend your life (presumption).

3. What duties does the virtue of charity help you fulfill?

The duty to love God with your whole heart because He is supremely perfect and all good and to love your neighbor as Jesus has loved you.

"If anyone says, 'I love God,' and hates his brother, he is a liar" [I John 4:20].

4. What does the command to love God with our whole heart imply?

It is evident from this Great Commandment that Jesus calls everyone of whatever rank or status to the fullness of the Christian life, which means high holiness, and to the goal of perfect love.

"The Lord Jesus, the divine Teacher and Model of perfection, preached holiness of life to each and every one of His disciples, regardless of their situation: 'You therefore are to be perfect, even as your heavenly Father is perfect'" [Matthew 5:48]. [Vatican Council II, The Church, par 40].

5. What are the best ways to show love of our neighbor?

a) The spiritual works of mercy: admonishing the sinner, instructing the ignorant, counseling the doubtful, comforting the sorrowful, bearing wrongs patiently, forgiving injuries, praying for the living and the dead;

b) The corporal works of mercy: feeding the hungry, giving drink to the thirsty, clothing the naked, ransoming the captive, harboring the harborless, visiting the sick, burying the dead.

6. Did Jesus give us a blueprint for a holy Christian life?

Yes, in the Sermon on the Mount [Matthew, chapters 5-7] and especially in the rules for happiness, the Eight Beatitudes [Matthew 5:3-10].

7. What are some sins against Christian charity?

Thinking, speaking, acting unkindly toward others, hatred, envy, causing discord, scandal, cooperating in the sins of others, refusing to forgive those who offend you.

NOTES

Lesson 42: **Fast and Abstinence**

Now Jesus, full of the Holy Spirit, returned from the Jordan, and was led by the spirit about the desert for forty days, being tempted the while by the devil. And he ate nothing those days; and when they were completed he was hungry. [Luke 4:1-2]

1. What is fasting?

Fasting means eating a smaller amount of food. The Church's law for a day of fasting prescribes —

a) only one full meal (with meat, if you wish);

b) two small meatless meals (small enough not to add up to another full meal);

c) no food between meals.

2. Who are obliged to fast?

Catholics when they become 18 years old until they reach 59. A sufficient reason excuses, such as illness, pregnancy, etc.

3. What are the days of obligatory fasting?

Ash Wednesday and Good Friday.

> *Fasting is one of the best forms of Christian discipline. No one should be satisfied with the bare minimum of fasting required by the Law.*

4. What is abstinence?

The Church's law of abstinence says that on certain days you may not eat meat.

5. What is meant here by "meat"?

The flesh of any warm-blooded animal or bird and soup or gravy made from such meat.

> *Fish foods are permitted on a day of abstinence. This includes lobsters, crabs, turtles, oysters, frogs, scallops, clams, etc.*

6. Who are obliged to abstain?

All Catholics who are 14 years old and over.

7. What are the days of obligatory abstinence?

Ash Wednesday and all the Fridays of Lent.

Therefore, on Ash Wednesday and Good Friday, both laws, fasting and abstinence, apply. On these days, no meat may be taken at the full meal.

NOTES

Prayers

1. The Sign of the Cross.

In the name of the Father, and of the Son, and of the Holy Spirit. Amen.

2. The Our Father.

Our Father, Who art in heaven, hallowed be Thy name. Thy kingdom come, Thy will be done on earth as it is in heaven. Give us this day our daily bread and forgive us our trespasses as we forgive those who trespass against us and lead us not into temptation, but deliver us from evil. Amen.

3. The Hail Mary.

Hail Mary, full of grace, the Lord is with thee. Blessed art thou among women and blessed is the fruit of thy womb, Jesus. Holy Mary, Mother of God, pray for us sinners now and at the hour of our death. Amen.

4. The Apostles' Creed.

I believe in God, the Father Almighty, Creator of heaven and earth, and in Jesus Christ His only Son Our Lord, who was conceived by the Holy Spirit, born of the Virgin Mary, suffered under Pontius Pilate, was crucified, died and was buried. He descended into hell, the third day He arose again from the dead, He ascended into heaven, sitteth at the right hand of God the Father Almighty from thence He shall come to judge the living and the dead. I believe in the Holy Spirit, the Holy Catholic Church, the Communion of Saints, the forgiveness of sins, the resurrection of the body, and life everlasting. Amen.

5. Glory be to the Father.

Glory be to the Father, and to the Son, and to the Holy Spirit, as it was in the beginning, is now and ever shall be, world without end. Amen.

6. Act of Contrition.

O my God, I am heartily sorry for having offended You, and I detest all my sins, because I dread the loss of heaven and the pains of hell, but most of all, because they offend You, my God, Who are all good, and deserving of all my love. I firmly resolve with the help of Your grace, to confess my sins, to do penance and to amend my life. Amen.

7. Blessing before eating.

Bless us, O Lord, and these Your gifts, which we are about to receive from Your bounty, through Christ, Our Lord. Amen.

8. Thanks after eating.

We give You thanks for all Your benefits, O Almighty God, who lives and reigns forever. May the souls of the faithful departed through the mercy of God, rest in peace. Amen.

9. Act of Faith.

O my God, I firmly believe that You are one God in three Divine Persons, The Father, Son and Holy Spirit. I believe that Your Divine Son became man and died for our sins, and that He will come to judge the living and the dead. I believe these and all the truths, which the Holy Catholic Church teaches, because You have revealed them, Who can neither deceive nor be deceived.

10. Act of Hope.

O my God, relying on Your infinite goodness and promises, I hope to obtain pardon for my sins, the help of Your grace, and life everlasting, through the merits of Jesus Christ, my Lord and Redeemer. Amen.

11. Act of Love.

O my God, I love You above all things, with my whole heart and soul, because You are all good and worthy of all my love. I love my neighbor as myself for the love of You. I forgive all who have injured me and ask pardon from all whom I have injured. Amen.

12. Hail Holy Queen.

Hail Holy Queen, Mother of Mercy, our life, our sweetness and our hope! To you do we cry, poor banished children of Eve; to you do we send up our sighs, mourning and weeping in this valley of tears! Turn then most gracious Advocate, your eyes of mercy towards us, and after this our exile, show us the blessed fruit of your womb, Jesus. O clement, O loving, O sweet Virgin Mary.

13. The Confiteor.

I confess to Almighty God, to blessed Mary ever Virgin, to blessed Michael the Archangel, to blessed John the Baptist, to the holy Apostles Peter and Paul, and to all the Saints that I have sinned exceedingly in thought, word and deed, through my fault, through my fault, through my most grievous fault. Therefore I beseech blessed Mary ever Virgin, blessed Michael the Archangel, blessed John the Baptist, the holy Apostles Peter and Paul, and all the Saints to pray to the Lord our God for me. May Almighty God have mercy on me and forgive me my sins and bring me to life everlasting. Amen. May the Almighty and merciful Lord grant me pardon, absolution and remission of all my sins. Amen.

14. Memorare.

Remember, O most gracious Virgin Mary, that never was it known that anyone who fled to your protection, implored your help and sought your intercession was left unaided. Inspired by this confidence, I fly to you, O Virgin of virgins, my Mother. To you I come; before you I stand, sinful and sorrowful, O Mother of the Word Incarnate, despise not my petitions, but in your mercy hear and answer me. Amen.

15. Morning Prayers.

In the name of the Father, and of the Son, and of the Holy Spirit. Amen.

O Jesus, through the Immaculate Heart of Mary, I offer You all my prayers, works and sufferings of this day for all the intentions of Your Sacred Heart, in union with the Holy Sacrifice of the Mass throughout the world. I wish to gain all the indulgences attached to the prayers I shall say and to the good works I shall perform this day. Help me to stay away from sin today.

Our Father, Who art in heaven ...
Hail Mary ...
I believe in God ...
Glory be to the Father ... Acts of Faith, Hope and Love (Page 134), Angel of God, my guardian dear, To whom His love commits me here. Ever this day be at my side, to light and guard, to rule and guide. Amen.

O Mary, my Queen and my Mother, I give myself entirely to You. And to show my devotion to you, I consecrate to You this day, my eyes, my ears, my mouth, my heart and my whole being without reserve. Wherefore, since I am yours, O living Mother, keep me and guard me as your property and possession. Amen.

In the name of the Father, and of the Son, and of the Holy Spirit. Amen.

16. Evening Prayers.

In the name of the Father, and of the Son, and of the Holy Spirit. Amen.

Our Father ... Hail Mary ... I believe in God ... Glory be ... O my God, I thank You for Your benefits, especially which I have received today from Your bounty.

Give me the light to know what sins I have committed today and the grace to be sorry for them

[Now go over the day's activities and find out what sins you have committed today.]

ACT OF CONTRITION: O my God, I am heartily sorry for having offended You. I detest all my sins because I dread the loss of heaven and the pains of hell, but most of all because they offend You, my God, Who are all good and deserving of all my love. I firmly resolve with the help of Your grace to confess my sins, to do penance and to amend my life. Amen.

Jesus, Mary and Joseph, I give you my heart and my soul.

Jesus, Mary and Joseph, help me in my last agony.

Jesus, Mary and Joseph, may I breathe forth my soul in peace with you.

May the Lord bless me and bring me to life everlasting.

And may the souls of the faithful departed rest in peace. Amen.

In the name of the Father, and of the Son, and of the Holy Spirit. Amen.

17. Prayers for going to Confession.

O loving and merciful God, help me to make a good confession. Help me to know my sins so that I may be able to tell the Priest what sins I have committed and how often I have committed them. Give me a deep sorrow for all my sins, and give me the help necessary not to sin again.

[Now look into your memory and see what sins you have committed since your last Confession; and how many times you committed each sin.]

O my God, I am heartily sorry for having offended You, and I detest all my sins because I dread the loss of heaven and the pains of hell but most of all because they offend You, My God, Who are all good, and deserving of all my love. I firmly resolve with the help of Your grace, to confess my sins, to do penance and to amend my life. Amen.

18. Prayer after Confession.

O Almighty and Merciful God, I wish to thank You for all the blessings which You have given me but especially for this one. Give me the strength necessary to overcome temptations and to be always faithful to You. I wish to renew the promises I made when I was baptized, and from this moment I give myself entirely to Your love and service. Let nothing in life or death separate me from You. Through Jesus Christ, our Lord. Amen.

NOTES

The Mysteries of the Rosary

The Rosary is a prayer in which you think on events in the life of Jesus and of His Blessed Mother. These events are called *Mysteries*. The Mysteries are divided into three groups:

THE JOYFUL MYSTERIES

1. THE ANNUNCIATION. The Angel Gabriel brings God's message to Mary.
2. THE VISITATION. Mary visits her cousin Elizabeth.
3. THE NATIVITY. Jesus is born in Bethlehem.
4. THE PRESENTATION. Jesus is presented in the Temple.
5. THE FINDING IN THE TEMPLE. Jesus is found in the Temple.

> *Biblical References:* (1.) *Luke 1:30-31, 38, Matthew 1:21, Isaiah 7:14;* (2.) *Luke 1:41-42, John 3:16;* (3.) *Luke 2:7, 14, Isaiah 9:5;* (4.) *Luke 2:23, Exodus 13:2, 1st Corinthians 2:9;* (5.) *Luke 2;46-49.*

THE SORROWFUL MYSTERIES

1. THE AGONY IN THE GARDEN. Jesus sweats blood.
2. THE SCOURGING AT THE PILLAR.
3. THE CROWNING WITH THORNS.
4. CARRYING OF THE CROSS. Jesus carries His cross.
5. THE CRUCIFIXION. Jesus dies on the cross.

> *Biblical References:* (1.) *Matthew 26:37-39, 46, Luke 22:44;* (2.) *Luke 18:33, John 19:1, Isaiah 53:4;* (3.) *Matthew 27:29, Mark 15:17-18;* (4.) *Matthew 27:31-32, 16:24, Isaiah 53:7;* (5.) *Luke 23:33, John 19:16-18.*

THE GLORIOUS MYSTERIES

1. THE RESURRECTION. Jesus rises from the dead.
2. THE ASCENSION. Jesus ascends into heaven.
3. THE DESCENT OF THE HOLY SPIRIT upon the Apostles.
4. THE ASSUMPTION. The Virgin Mary is taken up to heaven.
5. THE CORONATION. Mary is crowned Queen of heaven and earth.

> *Biblical References:* (1.) *Acts 3:15, Matthew 28:5-6, Mark 16:5-6;* (2.) *Luke 24:50-51, Mark 16:19, Acts 1:2;* (3.) *Acts 2:1-4, Romans 15:13, 8:2, John 3:5-6, 16:13-14.*

I believe in God, the Father Almighty, Creator of heaven and earth; and in Jesus Christ, His only Son, our Lord; Who was conceived by the Holy Spirit, born of the Virgin Mary, suffered under Pontius Pilate, was crucified, died, and was buried. He descended into hell; the third day He arose again from the dead; He ascended into heaven, sitteth at the right hand of God, the Father Almighty; from thence He shall come to judge the living and the dead. I believe in the Holy Spirit, the holy Catholic Church, the communion of saints, the forgiveness of sins, the resurrection of the body, and life everlasting. Amen.

Our Father, Who art in heaven, hallowed be Thy name, Thy kingdom come, Thy will be done on earth as it is in heaven. Give us this day our daily bread and forgive us our trespasses as we forgive those who trespass against us, and lead us not into temptation. But deliver us from evil. Amen.

Hail Mary, full of grace! The Lord is with thee: blessed art thou amongst women, and blessed is the fruit of thy womb, Jesus. Holy Mary, Mother of God, pray for us sinners, now and at the hour of our death. Amen.

Glory be to the Father, and to the Son and to the Holy Spirit, as it was in the beginning, is now and ever shall be, world without end. Amen.

The Hail Holy Queen

Hail Holy Queen, Mother of Mercy, our life, our sweetness and our hope! To thee do we cry, poor banished children of Eve; To you do we send up our sighs, mourning and weeping in this valley of tears! Turn, then, most gracious Advocate, your eyes of mercy towards us, and after this, our exile, show unto us the blessed fruit of thy womb, Jesus. O clement, O loving, O sweet Virgin Mary!

Pray for us, O holy Mother of God. That we may be made worthy of the promises of Christ.

Let us pray. O God, whose only-begotten Son, by His life, death and resurrection, has purchased for us the rewards of eternal life, grant, we beseech Thee, that meditating on these mysteries in the most holy Rosary of the Blessed Virgin Mary, we may imitate what they contain, and obtain what they promise, through the same Christ, our Lord. Amen.

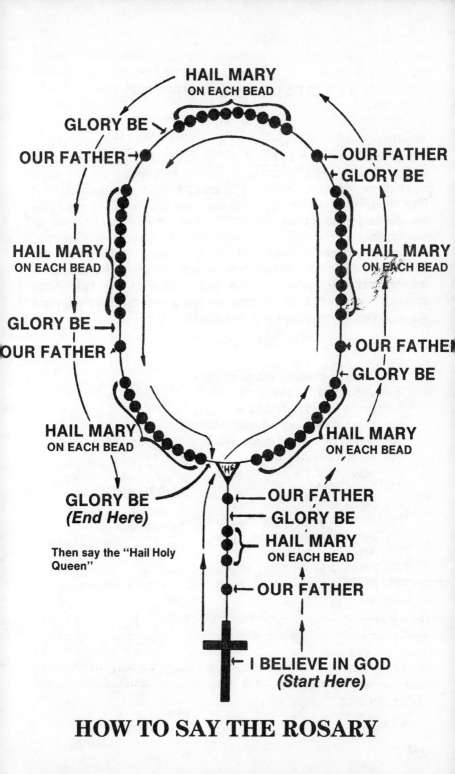

HAIL MARY
ON EACH BEAD

GLORY BE

OUR FATHER →

OUR FATHER ←

GLORY BE

HAIL MARY
ON EACH BEAD

HAIL MARY
ON EACH BEAD

GLORY BE →

OUR FATHER

OUR FATHER

GLORY BE

HAIL MARY
ON EACH BEAD

HAIL MARY
ON EACH BEAD

GLORY BE
(End Here)

Then say the "Hail Holy Queen"

OUR FATHER

GLORY BE

HAIL MARY
ON EACH BEAD

OUR FATHER

I BELIEVE IN GOD
(Start Here)

HOW TO SAY THE ROSARY

THE STATIONS OF THE CROSS

The Stations of the Cross is a devotion which consists in following our Lord in spirit on His sorrowful journey from Pilate's palace to His death and burial on Mount Calvary. In the early days of the Church, Christians used to trace the steps our Lord took in carrying His cross, but since most people could not make the trip to Jerusalem, the Church instituted the devotion known as the Stations of the Cross. In every Catholic Church you will see fourteen pictures or carvings which help you to recall the principal events of Christ's last hours. "Making the Stations" means that you walk from the first Station to the fourteenth, pausing at each one to meditate on the scene represented. Here are the titles of the Stations of the Cross:

1st. Jesus is condemned to death
2nd. Jesus carries His Cross
3rd. Jesus falls the first time
4th. Jesus meets His afflicted Mother
5th. Simon of Cyrene helps Jesus to carry His Cross
6th. Veronica wipes the face of Jesus
7th. Jesus falls the second time
8th. The Daughters of Jerusalem weep over Jesus
9th. Jesus falls the third time
10th. Jesus is stripped of His garments
11th. Jesus is nailed to the Cross
12th. Jesus dies on the Cross
13th. Jesus is taken down from the Cross
14th. Jesus is buried in the tomb

NOTES

_____

_____

_____

_____

NOTES

The Supreme Roman Pontiffs

St. Peter of Bethsaida in Galilee, Prince of the Apostles, who received from Jesus Christ the Supreme Pontifical Power to be transmitted to his Successors, resided first at Antioch, then at Rome for twenty-five years where he was martyred in the year 64, or 67 of the common reckoning.

END OF PONTIFICATE, A.D.		END OF PONTIFICATE, A.D.		END OF PONTIFICATE, A.D.		END OF PONTIFICATE, A.D.	
St. Linus, M.	76	Sabinianus	606	Leo VIII	965	Innocent VI	1362
St. Anacletus or Cletus, M.	88	Boniface III	607	Benedict V	966	B.Urban V	1370
St. Clement, I, M.	97	St. Boniface IV	615	John XIII	972	Gregory XI	1378
St. Evaristus, M.	105	St. Deusdeditus or Adeodatus I	618	Benedict VI	974	Urban VI	1389
St. Alexander I, M.	115	Boniface V	625	Benedict VII	983	Boniface IX	1404
St. Sixtus I, M.	125	Honorius I	638	John XIV	984	Innocent VII	1406
St. Telesphorus, M.	136	Severinus	640	John XV	996	Gregory XII	1415
St. Hyginus, M.	140	John IV	642	Gregory V	999	Martin V	1431
St. Pius I, M.	155	Theodore I	649	Sylvester II	1003	Eugene IV	1447
St. Anicetus, M.	166	St. Martin I, M.	655	John XVII	1003	Nicholas V	1455
St. Soterus, M.	175	St. Eugene I	657	John XVIII	1009	Callistus III	1458
St. Eleuterius, M.	189	St. Vitalian	672	Sergius IV	1012	Pius II	1464
St. Victor I, M.	199	Adeodatus II	676	Benedict VIII	1024	Paul II	1471
St. Zephyrinus, M.	217	Donus I	678	John XIX	1032	Sixtus IV	1484
St. Callistus I, M.	222	St. Agathonus	681	Benedict IX	1044	Innocent VIII	1492
St. Urban I, M.	230	St. Leo II	683	Benedict IX	1045	Alexander VI	1503
St. Pontian, M.	235	St. Benedict II	685	Sylvester III	1045	Pius III	1503
St. Anterus, M.	236	John V	686	Gregory VI	1046	Julius II	1513
St. Fabian, M.	250	Conon	687	Clement II	1047	Leo X	1521
St. Cornelius, M.	253	St. Sergius I	701	Benedict IX	1048	Adrian VI	1523
St. Lucius I, M.	254	John VI	705	Damasus II	1048	Clement VII	1534
St. Stephen I, M.	257	John VII	707	St. Leo IX	1054	Paul III	1549
St. Sixtus II, M.	258	Sisinnius	708	Victor II	1057	Julius III	1555
St. Dionysius	268	Constantine	715	Stephen X	1058	Marcellus II	1555
St. Felix I, M.	274	St. Gregory II	731	Nicholas II	1061	Paul IV	1559
St. Eutychian, M.	283	St. Gregory III	741	Alexander II	1073	Pius IV	1565
St. Caius, M.	296	St. Zachary	752	St. Gregory VII	1085	St. Pius V	1572
St. Marcellinus, M.	304	Stephen III	757	B. Victor III	1087	Gregory XIII	1585
St. Marcellus I, M.	309	St. Paul I	767	B. Urban II	1099	Sixtus V	1590
St. Eusebius, M.	309	Stephen IV	772	Paschal II	1118	Urban VII	1590
St. Melchiades, M.	314	Adrian I	795	Gelasius II	1119	Gregory XIV	1591
St. Sylvester I	335	St. Leo III	816	Callistus II	1124	Innocent IX	1591
St. Mark	336	Stephen V	817	Honorius II	1130	Clement VIII	1605
St. Julius I	352	St. Paschal I	824	Innocent II	1143	Leo XI	1605
Liberius	366	Eugene II	827	Celestine II	1144	Paul V	1621
St. Damasus I	384	Valentine	827	Lucius II	1145	Gregory XV	1623
St. Siricius	399	Gregory IV	844	B.Eugene III	1153	Urban VIII	1644
St. Anastasius I	401	Sergius II	847	Anastasius IV	1154	Innocent X	1655
St. Innocent I	417	St. Leo IV	855	Adrian IV	1159	Alexander VII	1667
St. Zozimus	418	Benedict III	858	Alexander III	1181	Clement IX	1669
St. Boniface I	422	St. Nicholas I (the Great)	867	Lucius III	1185	Clement X	1676
St. Celestine I	432	Adrian II	872	Urban III	1187	B.Innocent XI	1689
St. Sixtus III	440	John VIII	882	Gregory VIII	1187	Alexander VIII	1691
St. Leo I (the Great)	461	Marinus I	884	Clement III	1191	Innocent XII	1700
St. Hilary	468	St. Adrian III	885	Celestine III	1198	Clement XI	1721
St. Simplicius	483	Stephen VI	891	Innocent III	1216	Innocent XIII	1724
St. Felix III or II	492	Formosus	896	Honorius III	1227	Benedict XIII	1730
St. Gelasius I	496	Boniface VI	896	Gregory IX	1241	Clement XII	1740
Anastasius II	498	Stephen VII	897	Celestine IV	1241	Benedict XIV	1758
St. Symmacus	514	Romanus	897	Innocent IV	1254	Clement XIII	1769
St. Hormisdas	523	Theodore II	897	Alexander IV	1261	Clement XIV	1774
St. John I	526	John IX	900	Urban IV	1264	Pius VI	1799
St. Felix IV or III	530	Benedict IV	903	Clement IV	1268	Pius VII	1823
Boniface II	532	Leo V	903	B. Gregory X	1276	Leo XII	1829
John II	535	Sergius III	911	B. Innocent V	1276	Pius VIII	1830
St. Agapitus	536	Anastasius III	913	Adrian V	1276	Gregory XVI	1846
St. Silverius, M.	537	Landus	914	John XXI	1277	Pius IX	1878
Vigilius	555	John X	928	Nicholas III	1280	Leo XIII	1903
Pelagius I	561	Leo VI	928	Martin IV	1285	St. Pius X	1914
John III	574	Stephen VIII	931	Honorius IV	1287	Benedict XV	1922
Benedict I	579	John XI	935	Nicholas IV	1292	Pius XI	1939
Pelagius II	590	Leo VII	939	St. Celestine V	1296	Pius XII	1958
St. Gregory I (the Great)	604	Stephen IX	942	Boniface VIII	1303	John XXIII	1963
		Marinus II	946	B.Benedict XI	1304	Paul VI	1978
		Agapitus II	955	Clement V	1314	John Paul I	1978
		John XII	964	John XXII	1334	John Paul II, now reigning.	
				Benedict XII	1342		
				Clement VI	1352		

©Reprinted with permission from the *Official Catholic Directory*